# Censorship's Grave

## OBSERVATIONS, TOOLS, AND TIPS FOR TAKING THE INTERNET BACK FROM AUTOCRACIES

Philip G. Collier

## DEDICATION

To the people who persistently seek truth, break censorship barriers, and share what they know, because none of us are out of the darkness until all of us are out of the darkness.

# Table of Contents

# Chapter 1: A Universe of Talking Points

Imagine yourself taking a walk across your neighborhood, visiting friends - chatting about your daily lives and how things are going. With one, you talk about the season's weather, noting that there is not enough rain (or too much rain), not like it was years ago. With another, you make note of recent happenings up and down the street, and upcoming events at your place of worship. The last neighbor is interested only in politics, complaining that the super wealthy are not paying their fair share of taxes. On top of that, they are burning money on silly vanity projects which could pay for a thousand road and bridge repairs. None of that is unusual.

Suppose, however, that after you moved on, your friends were visited by a "neighborhood manager," who verified their identities on a list and asked questions to verify that you really did talk about weather, church activities, and taxes. Suppose you went for a stroll to visit the same people a week later, finding that the government had posted a "watchful friend" by their doors and would not let you visit. You were shunned because you had discussed taxes, religion, or weather trends.

Imagine the shopkeepers in your town, with their offerings of products and services. How would you react if one day you went out for pizza, only to discover that your favorite shop, a top notch international brand, had been forcibly closed; replaced with a local knockoff, said to be "just as good." Not as good, and

1

replaced for nothing actually related to pizza. It was done because the sole ruling party had financial interests in the local brand and ideological differences with the foreign company.

As a customer, you could simply accept the new situation. You could also opt to complain to anyone who would listen. What would you think of your town if you were barred from shopping or dining because of your gripes about that ratty pizza shop run by well-connected business people?

Who decides what is taught to your children in school? Is the curriculum based on verifiable facts? Are the students instead being force-fed a curriculum based on ideology, with no regard for what is known to be true?

That is how censorship works, though the examples are simplified. In this book, "censorship" will refer to actions taken by national or regional governments on behalf of persons or groups who control said governments. Governments censor on behalf of the powerful: ruling families, political parties, religious institutions, corporations, or industries considered "too big to fail." Censorship is the process of monitoring and regulating the many forms of expression for the purpose of protecting powerful interests.

Most often, censorship is applied to text, speech, music, or art on political, religious, economic, scientific, or social topics. The powerful, within their areas of influence, have a narrative – a version of reality – protected by censorship.

An easy way to cope with censorship, followed by many, is to accept it, adapt, and try to enjoy a life free of contention. However, there is harm in adapting to censorship. To accept censorship is to allow autocrats to take something which is not theirs: the basic human right to express oneself freely and to access the expressions of others.

Censorship interferes with the vetting process by which truth is found, and without truth there cannot be progress. Censorship interferes with justice, and without justice there cannot be peace.

Tied to the right of free expression are a myriad of things we humans express about, such as how and where we live, work, worship, or who we love. Expression is tied to governance; whether we self-govern or are governed by an outsider, whether the governance is broadly for the people or for a small subset of the people.

On a global scale, we humans are in the midst of a grand conversation (sometimes termed a "culture war"), developing a consensus about who we are and how we will exist in the near and distant future. **We all need to participate in the conversation, but billions of us are being cut out of it.** With vast accumulations of money, weaponry, or both, autocrats intend to bend humanity according to their will with disinformation, protected by censorship, and enforced by police or military powers.

War is Peace
Freedom is Slavery
Ignorance is Strength

George Orwell

Mind you, disinformation is not accepted well when presented by a scowling, violent, profane enforcer. Lies are readily consumed if presented by attractive and friendly symbols of soft power. Disinformation of the most offensive kind is readily accepted if presented by well groomed, smartly dressed political pundits with carefully crafted talking points.

What are talking points? They are snippets of ideas set up to persuade you to believe a specific version of reality. Talking points give *a version* of why things are as they are, who is responsible, and where you fit into the situation. Talking points are singular items which, when brought together, support an ideology.

Talking points are abundant everywhere. Look and you will see them in advertising, news reports, graffiti, in talk shows, and spoken by coworkers and family members. Why do you have a job (or not)? Why is the summer or winter weather so extreme? Is it good or bad to allow foreigners to visit as tourists? Is immigration beneficial (or not)? Is it good or bad for women to vote? Should we support Ukraine's membership in the European Union? Should NATO defend Ukraine? Who may fish or extract oil from the South China Sea? Should all Chinese in the world be governed by the Communist Party? Are all people really created equal, or is humanity a hierarchy of races?

Talking points frame the questions we ask; they also offer conformative answers. Some talking points are adopted as national policies. How the talking points are applied is dependent on whether the audience is a captive one or if competing ideas are allowed.

Autocracies protect their positions with censorship, reinforced with police powers. It is a simple matter for dictators to declare the existence of a problem, cite an ideology or foreign enemy as the source, then ban any associated discourse or expression.

# Eldridge Cleaver

**There is no more neutrality in the world. You either have to be part of the solution, or you're going to be part of the problem.**

In more (or sometimes less) free countries, the citizens are subjected to extremely well funded persuasive campaigns, where talking points are used to assert positions or attack conflicting positions of other groups. Often the strategy of attack is to appear as "merely asking questions" or to "flood the venue with sewage" in order to cause doubt or inaction among voters or lawmakers.

Why is this happening, and why now? It has been happening for a while, actually, but is accelerating and becoming more intense with each advance in mass communication. It is a conflict between people who are seeking progress and enlightenment versus others who intend to preserve established structures of power.

Entrenched power has always been at war with enlightenment and progress. It was apparent during the fight over the theory of a heliocentric universe. It was apparent when Martin Luther broke away from the Catholic Church. It was apparent when the Scopes "Monkey Trial" took place, in opposition to growing knowledge of evolution. Recently, as genetics has shown us how similar we humans are to each other, entrenched interests (mostly racist and fascist) continue to argue that we are different.

At the time of this writing, experts are aware that gender is not a binary issue of being either male or female; it is a matter of both chromosomes and the brain. For example a small number of persons have an extra "Y" chromosome. Others may have variations of the "X" chromosome. In fact, females exist who have one missing "X" chromosome instead of a "XX" pair, and a few bear a "XXX" combination. Beyond chromosomes, brain development may steer people toward a gender identification which does not fit conventional definitions. Such truths are being violently rejected by people of far-right ideology, who have no interest in knowledge derived from reason and observation.

**James Baldwin**

**It took many years of vomiting up all the filth I had been taught about myself, and half believed, before I was able to walk on the earth as though I had a right to be here.**

As much as the printing press or radio enabled the rapid and massive communication of ideas, the internet dwarfs them by orders of magnitude. Enlightenment has accelerated, challenging peoples' ancient beliefs about governance, race, religion, and identity. Likewise, censorship and deliberately manipulated information have been applied to blunt the spread of enlightenment. It is a burden on human progress, as much backlash is based on beliefs and frameworks which are simply untrue.

Established wealth and power, held by specific groups of people, are behind all of the campaigns defending industries or parties which govern countries. They will shamelessly argue from any possible angle to prevent new knowledge or technologies from disrupting their realms. Consider these notably absurd positions:

- Cigarettes cannot be proven to cause cancer.

- Fossil fuels cannot be proven to cause global warming.

- Democracy is not suitable for Chinese people.

- Democracy is not suitable for Russian people.

- Democracy is not suitable for White Christian Nationalists.

- Billionaires are more qualified to govern than working-class military or community leaders.

The term "culture war" has often been used to describe the two competing factions in the United States – "conservatives" against "progressives." Such a view is too narrow to contain the real situation; on a global scale, people of conservative or nationalist culture are doing everything possible to isolate and eliminate people seeking to expand enlightenment and progress. Watch events in Iran, Hungary, the United Kingdom, Syria, China, Brazil, and Turkey. You will easily notice similar dynamics at work.

Enlightenment will win, because truth is thermodynamic. Once seen, truth cannot be unseen – just as a glass of wine tossed into the sea cannot be returned to its glass. Censorship is about putting the wine back in the glass. It has failed for hundreds of years, it will continue to fail.

The last event in which censorship was *almost* successful was a mass burning of the Talmud and other Hebrew manuscripts in France, during the year 1242. King Louis IX, like modern day culture warriors, acted without awareness that paper is merely a medium. Mediums can be destroyed, but the ideas they carry cannot. Does burning a mathematics book eliminate algebra? Does burning the Beatles' *Get Back Sessions* un-create *Acrosss the Universe*? Ideas endure and tend to ripple outward from their origins.

Burnings of media have happened since the attempted Talmud eradication; all are theatrical expressions of hostility, not effective acts of information control. Methods of reproducing information have outstripped the methods of suppressing it since the printing press was invented. Radio, electronic recording, and digital media all multiply information at rates orders of magnitude greater than the printing press.

Despite knowing that truth cannot remain forever hidden, a question remains as to how censorship and disinformation can be defeated. I cannot predict how people will be convinced to accept logic and reason. Millions of people are presently falling prey to the most absurd conspiracy theories, despite ample evidence refuting them.

What I do know is that mathematics, logic, and software engineering can be used to defeat any censorship barrier. Every, and I do mean every, barrier to information has a measure of permeability which may be exploited. It is the stuff of nightmares for dictators – that none of their weapons is perfect and may be used against them by a sufficiently patient and ruthless adversary.

In the chapters to follow, this book will discuss how propaganda, disinformation, and censorship barriers have been beaten by patient and ruthless people who believe that all persons should enjoy freedoms of thought and expression, which ripple outward to empower them in all other aspects of life.

# Chapter 2: Double Edged Mass Media

Each expansion of mankind's ability to communicate has had the effect of democratizing knowledge. As knowledge propagated among more and more people, their responses have been varied. Some would accept it without question while others, more skeptical, put it to the test. A few (and sometimes more) view democratized knowledge as a threat.

It is a good thing, and a natural thing, for people to share ideas and debate – to find what is true, and to disrupt untruth when it appears necessary. Termed "critical thinking," it is the exercise which leads to more literacy and greater awareness of all aspects of our world. Unsurprisingly, critical thinking often attracts backlash from the powerful, who do not want their narratives challenged.

Backlash generally takes the form of penalties imposed on leaders of disruptive movements, controls imposed on means of communication, and censorship of disruptive content. Backlash often has an accompanying component of disinformation and a counter-narrative against a new consensus. In other words, media alone does not discern truth from lies and may be used to argue either side of contentious issues.

Johann Gutenberg was not trying to change the world when he invented the mechanical printing press in 1440, but was instead seeking an efficient way to mass produce small printed items he could sell. What was new in his printing press, which leaped beyond similar tools developed elsewhere, was splitting *typesetting* and *printing* into separate processes and using a screw to apply pressure.

Historians believe the first paper was created around the year 200 B.C. in China, was spread by traders on the Silk Road, and further developed during subsequent centuries in the Middle East and northern Africa. Arabs were secretive about the process of making paper and did not promote the knowledge to Europeans. It was through the crusades that Europeans became aware of paper making methods. Spanish paper mills were first built around 1150 A.D., followed by mills in other countries.

Movable type was invented in China during the eleventh century, using clay and then wooden words – inked and pressed against paper. By the early thirteenth century, cast metal movable type had been used in Korea.

Gutenberg's critical breakthrough was using metal movable type, modern paper, and a new means of applying precise, even pressure: flat plates against a rotating screw. His invention was soon adopted for mass printing of bibles, scholarly works, and political pamphlets.

By the year 1465, printing presses were being used by the Catholic Church to print indulgences and pamphlets promoting a crusade against the Turks. In terms of items produced per unit of time or per worker, the printing press outperformed scribes by a measure of about 500 to 1.

It was not long before the Church began to fear that the printing press it used to further its interests could be used as a weapon by reformers within the Church, persons who would convey unsanctioned interpretations of the scriptures, or other adversaries. Pope Alexander I, in 1501, implemented what we today would call a licensing scheme: a prohibition against publishing any books without the Roman Catholic Church's permission, under penalty of excommunication.

The printing press was indeed put to effective use during the Protestant Reformation. On the last day of October, 1517, Martin Luther brought forth a list of *95 Theses* about Christianity and doctrines of the Church. He especially took issue with the notion that any Christian needed the Church as an intermediary between themselves and God. To him, it was clear that nothing stood between anyone and God. There was one baptism, one gospel, and a community of Christians who were all peers.

Also, Luther asserted that forgiveness for sins was something which could not ever be bought or earned. He was offended by the idea that the rich could commit sin, give money to the Church, be forgiven, and sin more if they could afford to. What was a destitute person to do? Be damned for being poor? The budding reformer argued that forgiveness was granted by God according to one's faith, not wealth or performative good works.

If not for the printing press, Martin Luther may have simply been a disgruntled monk who stirred dissent, was disciplined, and finally forgotten. But there *was* a printing press; Luther's ideas spread far and wide. He had broad enough support to begin the Lutheran Church – the first of many protestant denominations.

Initially, the *95 Theses* were published in Latin, primarily for persons educated and active in the Church. Subsequent publications were in German, then eventually in other languages.

In Luther's time, literacy was not widespread, amounting to less than ten percent in rural areas and up to near thirty percent in urban areas. It is tempting to argue that things are not much better in America's "Red" states, but that is an issue to argue in a separate book... Information from printed materials was spread within populations by spoken word. Literate persons within families or at public gatherings would read aloud to others, who would verbally continue the movement of knowledge. An interesting aspect of printed books being available in local languages (not strictly Latin), is that literacy rates began to increase. Despite low literacy rates, the *95 Theses* were found to have merit.

Luther made effective use of the printing presses available in Germany. Some writings were disseminated as tracts or pamphlets; other items went out as complete books.

Luther's *Sermon on Indulgences and Grace* was written shortly after the *95 Theses*, and spread especially quickly as it was published in German. It was addressed not to the Church's leadership, but specifically to the people, and it was the first "best seller" of printed books. Speaking directly to the people was as bold and incendiary a move as any twentieth century pirate radio broadcaster or twenty-first century blogger.

In the *Sermon*, Luther argued several points which stirred a strong response among the people:

- Grace cannot be bought, but is given by God for good works and sincere faith.

- Regaining God's grace after sin must come through confession, sincere suffering, and repentance.

- Indulgences are not based on scripture.

- Indulgences give a false sense of satisfaction.

- Clergy are greedy, scheming to build wealth.

- Giving money for the local church to help the poor is better than sending money to Rome for construction of St. Peter's Basilica.

As with publishers today, Luther had a few problems with piracy: low quality cheap knockoffs of his work, sold at cheap prices.

Martin Luther experienced life threatening conflict with the Catholic Church. Pope Leo X excommunicated him in January 1521. On April 17th and 18th, he stood before the Diet of Worms, an assembly convened by Emperor Charles V, in Worms, Germany, where he was accused of heresy for his writings and commanded to recant or face the penalty of death. Luther was defiant, refusing to recant and boldly challenging the authorities to prove his assertions wrong.

After making his stand in Worms, Luther was taken into hiding, living for nearly a year in Wartburg, under the protection of Fredrick III. Luther continued to write, although his work was banned by Charles V in May of 1521. The pope and emperor were church and state, respectively, operating in lock step. Their rule set was simple: Luther's writings contradicted the Catholic Church, therefore they were outlawed. In response, Luther continued to publish, but under a pseudonym. When the *Index Librorum Prohibitorum* ("Index of Banned Books") was created in 1557, Luther's books were in its first iteration.

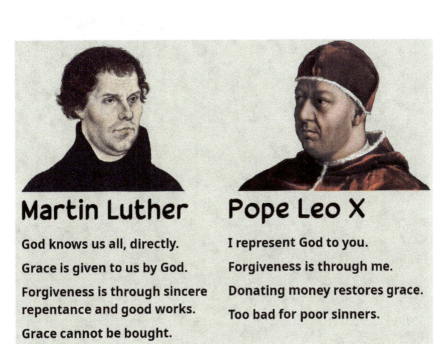

## Martin Luther

**God knows us all, directly.**

**Grace is given to us by God.**

**Forgiveness is through sincere repentance and good works.**

**Grace cannot be bought.**

## Pope Leo X

**I represent God to you.**

**Forgiveness is through me.**

**Donating money restores grace.**

**Too bad for poor sinners.**

Despite efforts to refute Lutheranism and prevent its spread, the new denomination spread throughout Europe, then to the Americas and is now worldwide.

Another notable flash point in the battle between conservatism and enlightenment was the discovery that our solar system was heliocentric (centered on the sun, not Earth).

Roundness was a property of our planet which was recognized by ancient Greeks in the sixth century B.C. By the fourth century, observers had begun trying to deduce the sizes of our Earth, Moon, and Sun. Observers compared the noontime angles of the sun in various locations, and used geometry to estimate Earth's size. They were not especially precise, but were generally on the right track. Aristarchus of Samos had gone as far as to assert that the sun was considerably larger than Earth and much farther away than the moon.

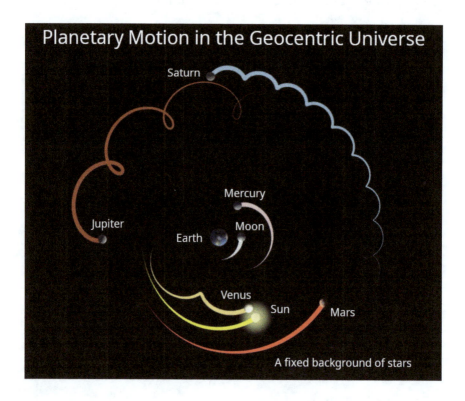

Awareness of these first astronomical sizes and distances was an early hint that scientists would need comprehension and skill to work comfortably with incredibly large (or small) numbers.

More than 1700 years after Aristarchus, Nicholas, Copernicus circulated first drafts of his revolutionary work, *De Hypothesibus Motuum Coelestium a se Constitutis Commentariolus*, in the year 1514. It is sometimes referred to as the "Little Commentary" in which he set forth an idea which explained the motions of the sun, planets, and stars. It was carefully worded in an effort to not arouse attacks from the Church. He published *De Revolutionibus Orbium Coelestium* ("On the Revolutions of the Heavenly Spheres") in the year 1543, setting in motion an arc of events which greatly advanced science and also challenged deeply held religious doctrines.

Giordano Bruno, was an early advocate of heliocentrism. He was a philosopher and former Dominican priest who found himself frequently at odds with the rigid mindset and intolerance of the Catholic Church. In the year 1584, he published *De l'infinito Universo e Mondi* (*"On the Infinite Universe and Worlds"*), a work which we now recognize as truly visionary. It contains perhaps the first speculation of the existence of exoplanets:

> In space there are countless constellations, suns and
> planets; we see only the suns because they give light;
> the planets remain invisible, for they are small and
> dark. There are also numberless earths circling around
> their suns, no worse and no less than this globe of
> ours. For no reasonable mind can assume that
> heavenly bodies that may be far more magnificent
> than ours would not bear upon them creatures similar
> or even superior to those upon our human Earth.

Bruno lectured and produced numerous writings challenging the thinkers and leaders of his time, arguing for more freedom of thought religious tolerance, and, without hesitation, attacking flaws in orthodox thought whenever he found them. Bruno was denounced and taken into custody and tried twice by the Roman

Catholic Inquisition – first in Venice, then in Rome.

The trial on charges of heresy lasted seven years. Bruno was steadfast; when it was demanded that he retract the statements he had made in the past, he refused. Pope Clement VIII ordered that Bruno receive the harshest of sentences for heresy and being *impenitent* and *pertinacious*. On the day of his formal sentencing, Bruno told his judges, "Perhaps your fear in passing judgment on me is greater than mine in receiving it." On February 17, 1600, with his tongue bound so that he could not speak, Giorano Bruno was executed by being set afire and burned to death.

Copernicus' concept of heliocentrism was further developed by Johannes Kepler, who found that the planets moved in elliptical orbits around the sun, with the sun at one focus and planetary speeds dependent on their distance from it. Galileo Galilei built telescopes and observed the planets in fabulous detail, discovering that some of them had moons orbiting them, as did Earth.

Galileo wrote *Sidereus Nuncius* ("Starry Messenger") in 1610. He was forbidden, in 1616, from defending or teaching heliocentrism, and later charged with heresy by the Roman Catholic Inquisition in 1633. He was threatened with torture and prison, but finally sentenced to house arrest, which was imposed until his death in 1642.

It is interesting to note that Church reformer Martin Luther criticised Copernicus' *De revolutionibus* when it was published, and the Catholic Church added it to the *Index Librorum Prohibitorum* 1616, for a duration of more than two centuries.

Censorship imposed by the Inquisition was not always applied uniformly. Historian Ada Palmer, during a lecture given for the University of Chicago in June 2021, described the Inquisition's actions as resembling an international syndicate of inquisitors working through various local governments. It mostly got what it wanted; when necessary, it could put its adversaries through multiple trials, as it did with Bruno and Galileo.

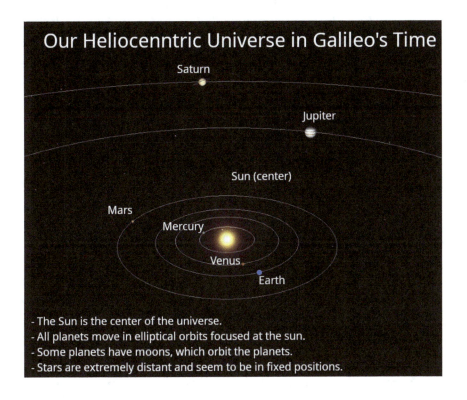

## Our Heliocenntric Universe in Galileo's Time

Saturn

Jupiter

Sun (center)

Mars

Mercury

Venus

Earth

- The Sun is the center of the universe.
- All planets move in elliptical orbits focused at the sun.
- Some planets have moons, which orbit the planets.
- Stars are extremely distant and seem to be in fixed positions.

What you do not see in the paragraphs above are accounts of the Church attempting to refute the basis of either Lutheranism or heliocentrism. The Church had enough power to simply demand obedience, without much need to counter argue its position on doctrines. It could excommunicate the disobedient, jail its more serious opponents, and prevent publication of so-called heretical literature.

Outside of Europe, the Inquisition's censorship was inconsistent. At the same time that missionaries were meticulously translating religious texts into indigenous languages in the Americas, campaigns existed in India which sought to eradicate spoken or written indigenous languages.

Even during the worst days of the Inquisition, censorship evasion was possible. As a first point, books banned by the Inquisition were not fully destroyed, but denied to the general population. Trusted professionals with a "need to know" could obtain an access license from a curator, after promising to ignore the specific content which was marked as banned.

For a second point, banned works were sometimes printed under misleading titles or authorship to hide their content from censors. When the authorities eventually discovered the prohibited material, publishers would change their books' titles and authorship again and continue publication.

There is a phenomenon, known today as the "Streisand Effect," in which attempts to hide information or prohibit access causes the opposite effect. It has existed under various names ever since the first human said, "Don't look!" to another, who immediately looked. The index of prohibited publications attracted plenty of attention from publishers seeking forbidden knowledge, which has always been profitable to publish.

Through the seventeenth and most of the eighteenth centuries, state censorship expanded in response to the proliferation of publications devoted to news and current events. Not quite the daily newspapers we know today, these early printings were released every few days and covered both foreign and domestic happenings.

Government censors checked and supervised the publishers, prohibiting materials which were deemed lewd or believed to be harmful to the state. Results varied from city to city; topics prohibited in one place could be permitted in another. A black market sought to meet demand created by the prohibitions.

A concept of "press freedoms" didn't burst into existence during the Early Modern period, but instead grew incrementally out of European states' refinement of regulations on publishers. There was a dynamic process of hashing out what could and could not be printed. The Star Chamber Decree is of importance, issued in 1585, during the reign of Queen Elizabeth I. It operated transparently, setting forth rules for publishing content as well as delegating duties and responsibilities for enforcement.

England was more progressive than other countries at the time, dividing powers between sections of the government and permitting a dialog to evaluate what the people's freedoms actually were.

The codified right of a person to express oneself and for others to access that expression was something which came into existence through a process of legal evolution. It is easy for respected philosophers or experts on the topic of governance to assert that a man should be free to speak his mind; much more difficult is crafting law applicable to all men, or to persons in general, which draws hard lines to protect expression.

The Magna Carta first came into existence in the year 1215. It set forth in writing a list of specific rights applicable to English citizens, affirmed first by King John I and amended over centuries. Its very first clause asserted that the English church was free to act without impairment, separately from the government. The government was limited in its power to imprison or otherwise punish citizens, requiring judgment of the accused in a fair process.

Notable also was the enumeration a right of "any man" offended by actions of the state to visit the crown or chief justice for redress of the grievances. The Magna Carta was an important step in recognizing the rights of persons. It was neither complete nor the end of the discussion, but it did establish the concept of specific privileges, immunities, and obligations in the relationship between a government and its citizens.

It is all well and good to know the motions of our planet and the many heavenly bodies. Establishing the knowledge as fact was neither easy nor bloodless. Even more contentious bodies of knowledge are those of evolution and genetics. Both deal with the development of living things we find in the world, including ourselves. They challenge our concepts of identity and how we developed into the beings we are today. Evolution and genetics are a direct challenge to deeply held religious doctrines.

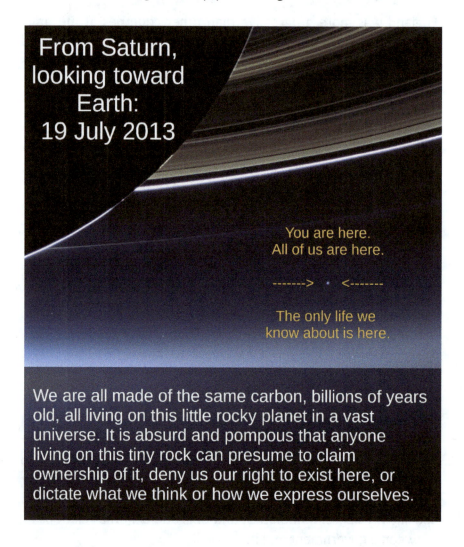

From Saturn, looking toward Earth: 19 July 2013

You are here.
All of us are here.

------->  ·  <-------

The only life we know about is here.

We are all made of the same carbon, billions of years old, all living on this little rocky planet in a vast universe. It is absurd and pompous that anyone living on this tiny rock can presume to claim ownership of it, deny us our right to exist here, or dictate what we think or how we express ourselves.

Charles Darwin published On *The Origin of Species* in the year 1859 and *The Descent of Man* in 1871. His theories directly challenged conventional teachings that life was created as many species and developed along a continuous path of improvement. Instead, Darwin came to believe that life evolved as adaptations to niche environments, developing as branches on a complex tree.

To him, species give rise to new species over time, according to the environments they occupied.

Alfred Russel Wallace explored areas of the world far from those visited by Darwin. Observing similarities and differences between various kinds of wildlife, he reckoned that present species come from older species, which come from yet older species.

To both men, there were fascinating connections between creatures which seemed very different. Manatees, which live in wetlands, have bones very similar to whales, which live in the sea. Butterflies and moths of different sorts have strangely similar structures in their exoskeletons and wings. Yet more strange was how they bore resemblance to fossilized remains of species which lived millions of years before.

All living things seemed to branch out as immense families within which there was variation. Survival of any species depends on how well it – with its variations - fits with its environment. Over time, species go out to occupy other environments, continuing to change as it lives under different conditions. Other species, if not compatible or able to adapt to new environments, die off.

The theory of evolution, as set forth by Darwin and Wallace, was gradually accepted by the educated as the most reasonable *scientific* explanation of the diversities and similarities of life. It was seen as heretical and threatening to those with a vested interest in traditional religious explanations of how the species came to be. The new theory was contrary to a deeply held concept of the *Great Chain of Being*, which asserted that a hierarchy existed, with God at the top and subordinate links extending down through the races of humans, other life, to a bottom level of minerals.

A great many schools would not teach evolution to their students. Most notably in the United States, and to a lesser extent, in other places with large numbers of fundamentalist believers in the Abrahamic religions, the concept of human evolution was offensive and heretical.

At the core of why evolution was rejected is this: that humans came from primates, as did monkeys and apes. Evolution conflicts with the *Book of Genesis*, which stipulates that mankind was created by God – in his image – separate from and above all other life. States in the American Bible Belt (mostly associated with the former Confederacy), were especially hostile to accepting and teaching evolution because it challenged not only the accepted human origin story, but white supremacy over other races.

# The Butler Act

**PROPOSED:**      John W. Butler, January 21, 1925
**VOTE TALLIES:**  House: 71 to 6; Senate: 24 to 6
**SIGNED:**        Governor Austin Peay, March 21, 1925
**REPEALED:**      May 18, 1967

**TEXT:**
BE IT ENACTED BY THE GENERAL ASSEMBLY OF THE STATEE OF TENNESSEE, That it shall be unlawful for any teacher in any of the Universities, Normals and all other public schools of the State which are supported in whole or in part by the public school funds of the State, to teach any theory that denies the story of the Divine Creation of man as taught in the Bible, and to teach instead that man has descended from a lower order of animals.

**PENALTY:**       No less than $100 nor more than $500

**CHALLENGE:**     Tennessee v. John Thomas Scopes
                   (a.k.a The Scopes "Monkey Trial")

John Butler was elected to the Tennessee House of Representatives in the year 1922, after campaigning on a platform of advocating for rural farmers and "protecting the children" from secular teachings such as the theory of evolution. Butler won the election. In 1924, he wrote the legislation which would become known as the Butler Act, prohibiting the teaching of "any theory that denies the story of the Divine creation of man as taught in the Bible, and to teach instead that man has descended from a lower order of animals."

When Butler submitted his proposed law, it passed quickly and quietly in the state house, with no public hearings or floor debates. Before the senate vote, the public became aware of it, engaging in vigorous debate for and against passage. It passed in the senate and was quickly signed into law by Governor Austin Peay, who offered dismissive comments that the law was no big deal and not likely to be enforced.

I offer a suggestion here and now to all readers to be wary when elected representatives are dismissive about anything they sign or support during a vote. When they sign or vote on any matter, it is serious; "no big deal" is always a big deal.

Be aware that the Butler Act was indeed a law contrary to the Constitution's First Amendment, which prohibits the U.S. congress from passing laws respecting religion. States could get away with legislation such as the Butler Act until the establishment clause was *incorporated,* meaning tested at the Supreme Court and found to be applicable to states. That did not happen until *Everson v. Board of Education* in 1946.

Contrary to what one may discern from the vote tallies in the Tennessee senate and house of representatives, there was opposition to the Butler Act, most importantly from the American Civil Liberties Union. The ACLU would argue on behalf of teacher John T. Scopes, who was cited for teaching evolution shortly after the law was enacted.

It was said to be the "trial of the century," with updates telegraphed out to newspapers and live coverage carried on radio stations. Proponents of the Butler Act gave speeches at rallies.

Preachers in churches bellowed and barked that it was necessary to fight the creeping influence of godless science into the faithful rural heart of America.

John T. Scopes

Defense lawyer Clarence Darrow gave a fiery and energetic argument against imposition of religious tests for school curricula. He argued:

> What we find here is as bold and as brazen an attempt to destroy learning as was ever made in the Middle Ages. The only difference is we have not provided that Mister Scopes should be burned at the stake. But

there is time for that, Your Honor; we must approach these things gradually.

We have been informed that the legislature has the right to prescribe study in the public schools. Within reason, they no doubt have. But the people of Tennessee adopted a piece of legislation that says, "You shan't teach any theory on the origin of man except the divine account as contained in the Bible." No legislature is strong enough to pick a book as being divine. The state of Tennessee has no more right to teach the Bible as the divine book than that the Koran is the one, or the Book of Mormon, or the books of Confucius, or the Buddha, or the essays of Emerson...

...What is the Bible? It is a book primarily of religion and morals. It is not a book of science – never was and never was meant to be. There is nothing prescribed that would tell you how to build a railroad or a steam boat, or how to make anything that would advance civilization. It's not a book on biology. They know nothing about it. They thought the earth was created four thousand and four years before the Christian era. We know better. I doubt if there is anyone in Tennessee who doesn't know better.

In America, there are at least 500 different sects or churches, all of which quarrel with each other on the importance or non-importance of certain things, or the construction of certain passages. Who is the chief mogul who will tell us what the Bible means? No criminal statute can rest that way! There is not a chance for it. The Butler Act is a criminal statute, and every criminal statute must be plain and simple.

I am a pseudo scientist, and I believe in evolution. Can a legislative body say to somebody like me that, "You cannot read a book, take a lesson, or make a talk on science until you first find out whether you are saying anything against Genesis?" It could, if it were not for the work of Thomas Jefferson, which is woven into EVERY state constitution, including this one, and which says, "No preference shall be given to any religion by law."

Yet, here we have the state of Tennessee teaching evolution for years. Along comes somebody who says we have to believe it the way they believe it, and they publish a law – the Butler Act – inhibiting learning! It makes the Bible the yardstick to measure every man's intellect, to measure every man's intelligence, to measure every man's learning...

Darrow smashes any possible basis for convicting Scopes. For his closing, he bites down and shakes the court like an angry dog, arguing that if permitted, the attack on enlightenment has no logical limits. Why stop at teaching evolution in schools? Why not go all the way?

...Your Honor knows the fires that have been lighted in America to kindle religious bigotry and hate. If today you can take a thing like evolution and make it a crime to teach it in the public schools, tomorrow you can make it a crime to teach it in the private schools, in the hustings, or in church. At the next session, you can ban books and newspapers. If you can do one, you can do the other.

After a while, Your Honor, it's the setting of man against man and creed against creed, until with flying banners and beating drums, we are marching backwards to the sixteenth century, when bigots burned the men who dared to bring any intelligence, enlightenment, and culture to the human mind!!

Scopes was convicted after a jury deliberation of about nine minutes and fined USD $100. His conviction was reversed on a technicality by the state supreme court. The Butler Act was never enforced again and similar laws in 22 other states were defeated.

Clarence Darrow

Scopes was not the end of contention over evolution, however, as subsequent conservative movements have repeatedly squared off against the theory. In more recent times, "Intelligent Design" and other competing theoretical frameworks have been offered as substitutes – or at least to muddy the waters and cause doubt in evolution. Darwin and Wallace were an intermediate waypoint, neither starting nor ending, on the path of understanding how life varies and evolves.

Groups will often attempt to use government for suppression of information they oppose. However, acting through private institutions or commercial enterprises is sometimes more successful. Private schools, subscription newspapers, and closed churches or social organizations can assert control in ways prohibited to the government.

Scientists have developed a deep understanding of genetics, from discovery of the double-helical DNA molecule, to mapping the genomes of humans and other life forms. Teaching and managing the knowledge has been fought by the usual suspects: institutions supported by people who hope to preserve a religious, cultural, and racial hierarchy.

Brainwashed citizens can be counted on to do their part in furtherance of censorship. It is popular to cite examples of protests against Western media in China or North Korea. They have happened plenty of times. Here is a lesser known example from the autumn of 1974. In Kanawha County, West Virginia, a conflict took place known as the "Textbook War." It is perfectly illustrative of the fact that censorship always has a context, never existing in a vacuum. What's more, a group radicalized on religion, politics, or both, can attack the freedom of expression as vigorously as any government actors.

Since the early 1900s, and especially after school desegregation in the 1950s, schools in fundamentalist Christian areas had used textbooks teaching a world view similar to that held by the people. Often, there was minimal emphasis on contentious topics like evolution. Nor was there much cultural or racial diversity. Content was typically favorable to right wing viewpoints - filtered by advocacy groups such as the United Daughters of the Confederacy (UDC).

How far right leaning is the UDC? Consider that the UDC framed the Civil War as an act of aggression by the Union against a noble and patriotic alliance of Southern states. Consider that the UDC is responsible for the proliferation of early twentieth century memorials and statues devoted to the Confederacy.

Implementing a curriculum portraying the United States as a multicultural democracy with a complex political and religious dynamic was patently unacceptable to the people of Kanawha County. People opposed to the new, realistic, and progressive curriculum protested. They yelled and got into fist fights during school board meetings, fired guns at opponents, and bombed schools. In the end, the progressive text books were used. Some students transferred to private schools while others stayed. Some teachers followed the new curriculum while others ignored it and refused to cover disputed topics.

As with the American Civil War, the end is never really the end. Parents and school board members continue to clash today over teaching the Lost Cause myth. They argue about evolution, biology, sex education, and civil rights.

Censorship is not specifically a tool for fighting science or history. Rather, scientific and historical knowledge are disruptive to the status quo, revealing truths which had been hidden – truths refuting myths accepted as factual.

Such is the sensitivity of people topics which touch upon identity or relate to foundations of political or religious power, that they can drive high emotions, legislation, and sometimes spur violence which takes place over long time spans - multiple decades, if not centuries.

Mass media grew by orders of magnitude through expansion of radio, television, and creation of the internet. A mass media so large cannot be effectively censored, though nations make incredible efforts to do so. Aware that censorship is less effective generally, and far less effective where people have more freedom of expression, manipulators have found ways of weaponizing disinformation to achieve their goals.

# Chapter 3: Information Warfare

In 1644, John Milton published *Areopagitica*. It was a work of protest, complaining about governmental book licensing requirements. He argued that truth is more powerful than falsehoods, and that a nation's intellect and moral sense needs free communication between the people. It could be that Milton had a sense that information wants to be free and needs interconnectivity between people. In the same way that the addition operation 2 + 2 = 4 has no attribute of boundary, being true everywhere, neither does information.

Judging from history since Milton put his words on paper almost 380 years ago, I would say that he is largely correct. However, two things are clear. Truth can be perceived as threatening. Also, *ideas not true* may be used to mislead people for years and decades. Truth wins eventually, but it must compete with flawed and incomplete knowledge. Truth must also compete with outright falsehoods intended to control, manipulate, and sometimes destroy populations of people.

If in doubt about the destructive and enduring effects of brainwashing and suppression of truth on a large scale, look into rhetoric used to support the transatlantic slave trade, elimination of native peoples of the Americas, or twentieth century genocides in Europe, Africa, and Southeast Asia. Those events were *all* supported by arguments that the upheavals were necessary for *the greater good*. Not for the general greater good of humanity, but the greater good of specific people, as bound in a nationalistic or tribal sense.

The engineering of mass communication continued to expand through the nineteenth century. As expected, printing presses became more precise, robust, and less expensive, but new technologies were also created, hinting at great things to come.

Invention of the telegraph enabled news and messaging to travel orders of magnitude faster between locations. It required some time to send messages, using hand keys, and multiple hops to cover long distances – but telegraphy was more fast and flexible than sending messages by courier. As shipping and travel by roads and waterways increased, so did the spread of printed texts.

If charted on paper, with one axis representing the number of people reached by information and the other axis representing time, progress follows a pattern of mostly small increments and a few large jumps. With respect to mass communication, the curve steepens its upward slope when new technologies are created *and* adopted. The curve is flattened as limits are reached, which prevent more people from accessing higher volumes of mass communication.

What are common factors which limit communication?

- Literacy – ability to speak or read one or more languages
- Technology – tools for communication: presses, paper, telegraphy, radio, television, or computers
- Cost – affordability of books, papers, or electronics
- Access – availability of books, papers, radio, TV, internet
- Content – restrictions on what is written or talked about
- Censorship – deliberate suppression of literacy, technology, access, or content

Indeed, there have been plenty of people in the industrialized world who, for reasons listed above, were not direct users of mass communication. During the American Civil War, news of battles or notable casualties traveled by telegraph and courier. News would trickle from top tier consumers of information, through the various levels of informed people, and finally pass by word of mouth to people of limited access to information.

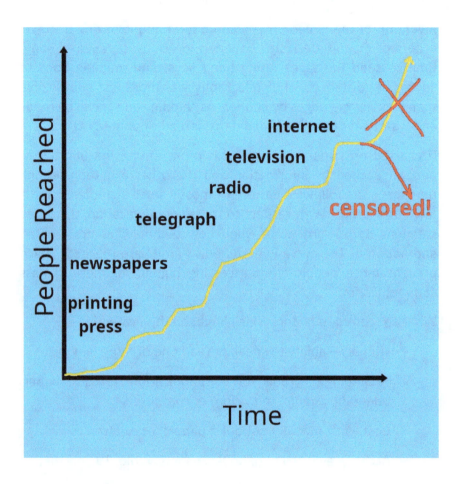

When President Abraham Lincoln died on the morning of April 15th, 1865, of wounds inflicted by his assassin, news had spread throughout the country before the end of the day, by telegraph. Newspapers carried the news over the following days. It took several weeks for word of his death to reach distant countries in the eastern hemisphere.

Oddly, newspapers were not especially clear about the fact that

Lincoln had died, or that he was killed by a gunshot to the head. Articles discussed the play he was attending, distinguished guests who were present, and things said by the killer. And, by the way, Lincoln was mortally wounded... One needed to read multiple articles in order to get a clear understanding of what had happened.

For most people at that time, they were told of what was going on by someone who was told by someone else, who may have read of events in a book or newspaper. Their awareness of the world was composed of a patchwork of indirect knowledge. Likewise, the world's awareness of any individual was small to nil, and certainly indirect.

Science fiction writers of the late nineteenth century were beginning to speculate on a future mass media, where individuals could access up-to-the-minute news or to be in audio / visual contact with others in distant places.

Mark Twain published a work in 1898, titled *From The London Times In 1904*, in which a death row prisoner, Mr. Clayton, has access to a device enabling him to see and talk to others around the world. Using a "Telectroscope," he discovers that the man he was condemned for murdering is actually alive and well. Unfortunately, the justice system would not rescind Clayton's death sentence and it was carried out.

Years before Twain's novel was published, another writer, Edward P. Mitchell, published a science fiction romance novel set in future year 1937. *The Senator's Daughter* tells a tale of love and division over issues of politics and race. A description is given in the novel of a device which prints a stream of current news, focused on topics selected by the user.

Twain and Mitchell hinted at a future social media and usenet, respectively, with the user in control and no hint that governments would block access to things or throttle the flow of information. Censorship was simply not a relevant part of the novels' plots.

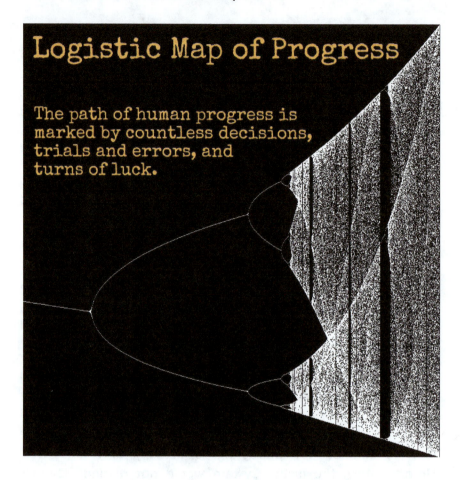

Communication technology developed rapidly through the latter nineteenth century. Even while telegraph wires were being strung between cities, and later between countries, inventors were developing voice telephony. Alexander Graham Bell patented a functioning telephone in 1876; within a year he had created the Bell Telephone Company and demonstrated voice communication over several kilometers, using modulated direct current over telegraph wires.

Nearing the end of the nineteenth century, wireless telegraphy had not only been invented, but was developing rapidly. Guglielmo Marconi received his first patent for wireless apparatus in 1896. Transmissions were crude and of short range at first, but

Marconi demonstrated increasingly long range capabilities with time, exceeding 300 km by the year 1901. Lee DeForest and others were creating a means of communication which would soon be superior to hard wired telegraphy. Telephone and telegraph communications increased mankind's ability to communicate from point to point, but not on a massive scale and not at a low enough enough expense to be easily available to the common man.

Things changed in a major way when AM radio was developed. A lot of scientists and engineers were in pursuit of the key technology which would make wireless signals capable of carrying voice and music. I will cite Edwin Howard Armstrong as the key inventor and most gifted development engineer who repeatedly created or perfected technologies necessary for radio broadcasting to exist. He even brought FM radio from a misunderstood theoretical construct into a practical system for broadcasting noise-free high fidelity music and voice programming.

A new visual medium, photography, was being created in the early 1800s. Development of the technology was a slow, decades long process involving chemistry, optics, materials science, wrought by inventors in multiple countries. Photography proved to be a valuable tool for journalists, artists, historians, and others who sought images to accompany their written words.

To top off this cauldron of nineteenth century technological innovation, work to create a means of recording sound bore fruit in the phonograph, which was patented in 1878. As with photography, it expanded the volume of mass media, where people are able to inform, entertain, and argue. Mass media expanded in a proportion which hadn't occurred since the birth of the printing press. As new media space was created, people filled it with all sorts of human expression.

Let us now ask what this history has to do with censorship. It is this: mass communication had outpaced nation-states' ability to censor since invention of the printing press. For all of the severe punishments inflicted on heretics, information - whether good or bad - was available. Authorities could curate forbidden content and largely limit access, but eradication had become impossible. In reality, it was demand which dictated how fast and far information would spread.

Rolling into the twentieth century, authorities around the world now had multiple, rapidly growing, forms of media to target for monitoring and regulation.

While all countries practice censorship in some measure, it is the non-free or autocratic countries which rely on it the most. We have seen how, in the more free countries, contention can arise over topics such as school books, science, religion, or race - essentially issues of identity. Autocracies know such topics are sensitive among their people and manipulate them with it. Regimes tend to build a supporting narrative along these lines:

- A nationalist story of past greatness and heritage or of a lost empire which should be restored.

- A nationalist myth of innocence, meaning that the problems of a group of people come not from the autocratic regime, but from an enemy outsider.

- After greatness, a time of lost purity and national humiliation which must be avenged.

- A culture of not looking inward. People are discouraged from asking, "What is *our* true history and what are *we* doing now?"

- A cult of personality surrounding a strongman type of leader who is omnipresent, omnipotent, and infallible.

Censorship is used to protect the ideology of regimes by plucking out contradictory narratives. It is complementary to the regime's official narrative and its supporting pillars, as mentioned above. Abundant mass media, however, limits the effectiveness of pure censorship as the sole means of suppressing disruptive information. What autocracies have found to be effective is creating fear, uncertainty, and doubt around disruptive information by both blocking it and peppering the people with several competing alternatives. In other words, media must be flooded with distractions, noise, or pro-regime propaganda in an effort to make people divided and indecisive.

Competing information alternatives fall into two categories, misinformation and disinformation. Misinformation is changing the meaning or emphasis of information in a manner which makes it non-threatening. It is deflecting attacks by "spinning" the narrative. For example, if a new report from the United Nations cites global temperature increases as a cause for more stormy weather in temperate latitudes, lawmakers supporting the fossil fuel industry could cite the same report to argue that farmers in the north have longer growing seasons and more rain for farmlands. The spin would deflect attention from the increasing drought and loss of farmland within the tropics or rising sea levels which displace island populations.

I will use polite terms for disinformation: lies and bold faced lies. Specifically, it is information which is intentionally misleading or not true. When lawmakers and journalists gaze into television cameras and say, "People who entered the United States Capitol building on January 6, 2021 were peaceful visiting tourists," they are spreading disinformation (sometimes known as "telling lies"). When Russian news media report that Malaysian Airlines flight MH17 was shot down by a Ukranian Mig-29 fighter, then report later that the culprit was instead an Su-25, both instances are disinformation (sometimes known as "bold faced lies").

Perhaps the text in chapters to follow will need a more precise terminology for the coordinated usage of censorship and disinformation. Dr. Dan Kuehl, of the School of Information Warfare and Strategy at the National Defense University, in Washington, DC, is an expert on *information warfare*. Information warfare is defined as "a conflict or struggle between two or more groups in the information environment."

An information environment can be thought of as anywhere information is gathered, received, transmitted, processed, or acted upon. It encompasses any physical or virtual dimension where people chat, teach, argue, discuss, consider, make decisions, create, or consume information. It is where we listen to music, podcasts, or radio programming. It is any book shop, internet media site, or chat room. It is satellite and cable television. It constitutes internet forums, silly pastebin sites, and in darknet markets. An information environment is anywhere persons participate in expression.

Media manipulation is the soft face of antidemocratic power. A much harder face exists, in the form of harassment and violence directed against journalists, social media figures, and platforms where they are based. Directly applied state power against free expression takes the form of legal restrictions, prosecutions, and criminal penalties as severe as execution. Autocracies use a *broad* and *vague* rule set for censorship for minimal constraint in getting rid of opponents.

If you believe your bookstore is packed with propaganda, it could be due to a forced inventory of favorable books and magazines. If your social media is packed with people who only show pictures of their pets or praise the national leadership, it could be due to your friends and colleagues having no safe options to express anything else – or their writings being purged from the platform.

Understand that no information environment is perfectly neutral. *Your* information environment is skewed one way or another, as is mine. Even the most free and progressive countries have information environments which lean slightly, at least in the interest of public safety, without conducting information warfare.

Denmark and Sweden, for example, have rules regulating the publication and trade in materials containing drug usage, depicting sexual activity, criminal behavior, or building improvised weapons. Developed democracies apply *narrow* and *specific* censorship rule sets to address public health and safety without undue infringement on the basic right to participate in free expression.

A surprisingly large number of countries do intentionally manipulate their information environments in order to shape opinions and control their citizens. It is commonly believed that China, Iran, Russia, and North Korea maintain tight media controls. They do. However, a closer look at the world reveals a much longer list of countries where intentionally waged campaigns of censorship and disinformation happen. The *2020 Global Inventory of Organized Social Media Manipulation* found eighty-one such countries! Consider these statistics:

- 81 countries with large social media manipulation campaigns

- 48 countries with private firms managing media manipulation

- 90% of countries have strong and simultaneous pro-government and anti-opposition messaging in the media

- 73% of countries have media campaigns which use trolling and harassment to inhibit civic participation

According to Freedom House, an organization which studies trends in democracy and autocracy worldwide, media manipulation is increasing, spurred by a rise in antidemocratic behavior of not only governments but also certain populations of people. Independent journalism does best in countries which are more free; increasing autocracy has caused more people to not have access to media which is separate from their governments. Likewise, personal expression is becoming more restricted, trending inversely with autocracy.

V-Dem is another organization which studies governance trends in the world, with a huge data set of over 31 million items. Their *Democracy Report 2023* reports declining freedom of expression in 35 countries. V-Dem, like Freedom House, have found that primary targets of autocratic movements are academic freedom, cultural freedom, and freedom of expression.

Why do so many people accept so much censorship and media manipulation? Reasons vary in specifics from place to place, but the underlying motivation is similar: a lust for power and wealth, cloaked in religious devotion and / or ethnic nationalism. Often, a backlash against social change creates a favorable environment for for authoritarian governance. Authoritarians claim to their followers, "You are under attack! Only I will do what is necessary to protect you!"

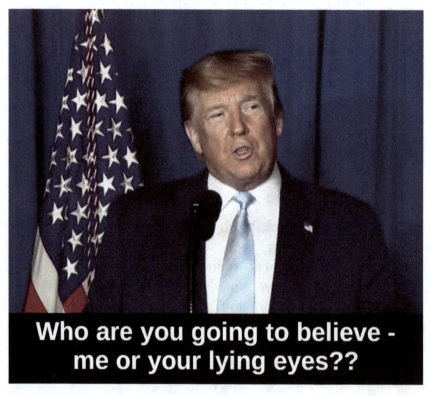

## Who are you going to believe - me or your lying eyes??

Authoritarians are charismatic, building a cult of people who go all-in to support their regime and adopt the supporting narratives listed above. In such an environment, a free media is intolerable. Free thought and expression would destroy the regimes; they depend for survival on information warfare. That's censorship within their borders and disinformation within other countries. Let us consider a few examples.

Led by Vladimir Putin, the Russian Federation is classified as a "non-free" country, with a very high level of media restriction, and few civil liberties. Russia is involved in a genocidal war against Ukraine, which is said to have no right to exist. Putin intends to establish a new Orthodox Christian empire of Slavic ethnicity. Any persons speaking contrary to official narratives put themselves at risk of prison or worse.

National media in Russia is regulated by Roskomnadzor, which has taken to blocking websites without going through the process of citing the operators or getting proper orders from a court. Independent media outlets, such as the Voice of America, Meduza, or the British Broadcasting Corporation, were blocked.

The People's Republic of China (PRC) has numerous issues of internal governance and contention over territorial boundaries. Both the PRC and Taiwan (the Republic of China) claim the same territory as "China," not having settled their civil war which dates back to 1945. Presently, there is no armistice, peace treaty, or consideration of a two-state solution. The PRC is staunchly Marxist, while Taiwan is governed democratically. Concurrently, there are potentially violent conflicts over territorial claims in seas to the east and south.

Closely tied with territorial claims is a nationalist belief that people of Chinese ethnicity, anywhere, should accept governance and be loyal to the ruling Communist Party.

Media of all types are highly regulated in the PRC. There are plenty of newspapers, vast bookstores, numerous high definition television channels, and radio stations galore. However, they all conform to official narratives. Foreign internet media is blocked. Shortwave radio broadcasts are either jammed with noise or multi-megawatt China Radio broadcasts.

Iran, Afghanistan, Saudi Arabia, and other Muslim majority countries have a different set of narratives requiring tight media control. They will all claim obedience to demands found in the Koran. Often, there is another layer of restrictions which protect the ruling families or political parties.

Censorship is often broad, with civil liberties extremely limited, especially for girls and women. Again, media is plentiful in quantity and narrow in content. Dozens and dozens of media sources exist, with mostly the same content repeated over and over.

How about the United States? Is there censorship? Is there information warfare? Yes to both questions.

There is an old adage which warns that people judge individuals by the allies with whom the individual associates. Intelligence experts make such judgments with a method called *relational algebra*. It turns out that relational algebra is a great tool for classifying people according to talking points they use. Compare and follow trends in argumentation by public figures to discover their concealed links and allegiances. If any sets of talking points correlate, there are connections between the people using them.

As in other Western countries, the USA incorporates freedoms of speech, peaceful assembly, and religion into its national constitution. States are bound to respect the constitution and to provide equal protection of the law to *all persons* within their jurisdictions. The obligations are not being met, most specifically in states with majority *Republican Party* governance.

As these words are being written, lawmakers in the state of Florida are promoting a bill which would require journalists, under penalty of law, to add their names to a registry if they create content about certain state officials. Jason Brodeur introduced bill *SB1316*, which appears curiously similar to the *Media Act* in Viktor Orban's Hungary.

Texas lawmaker Steve Toth is pushing a bill, *HB 2690*, requiring internet service providers to block access to websites providing information about certain women's reproductive health issues.

Numerous states are restricting content in libraries related to American history, the Civil Rights movement, evolution, genetics, and gender identification. Under the banner of combating foreign malware and hacking risks, members of the national congress have submitted bills *S.686 and H.R.1153,* which would allow the government to ban applications and online services. Accessing those services through circumvention tools would be punishable with fines and prison terms.

Russia has been waging an information war against the USA for several years, especially since the 2016 election race between Donald Trump and Hillary Clinton. Vast amounts of misinformation and disinformation have been spewed throughout the information environment. AM talk radio, social media, newspapers, and television news outlets have been a part of the operation.

During any given hour of the day, vast amounts of social media items are freshly posted, focused on three goals. First, to argue about current issues in a way which enrage people of right wing ideology, motivating them to vote and act against libraries, school boards, and local legislatures. Second, draw a bleak picture for people of progressive or liberal ideology, destroying motivation and causing them to not vote or engage in other activism. Third, to destroy trust between people as well as in their government and institutions.

Deep state conspiracy theories, the Qanon movement, vaccine disinformation, and "Big Lies" about the 2020 election are all part of the information war. It seems that Russia needs a weakened and distracted America, which will not put up significant resistance to Russia's empire building. Russia allies Iran and the PRC also benefit from reduced opposition to their respective anti-democratic agendas in the Middle and Far East.

However, the information war is not solely about Russia, Iran, and

China. A budding multinational *white power* movement has hated America's gradual shift toward pluralism and cultural diversity. They have fought it every step of the way since the Sectional Crisis in the 1850s, leading up to the Civil War.

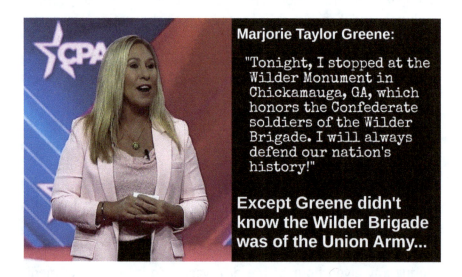

**Marjorie Taylor Greene:**

"Tonight, I stopped at the Wilder Monument in Chickamauga, GA, which honors the Confederate soldiers of the Wilder Brigade. I will always defend our nation's history!"

**Except Greene didn't know the Wilder Brigade was of the Union Army...**

White power advocates, such as former president Donald Trump, congresspersons Paul Gosar, Marjorie Taylor Greene, and Lauren Boebert, all make statements to mass media which are at least incorrect, if not outright falsehoods. They are enthusiastic advocates for Russia and embrace its acts of information warfare. In fact, they defend Russia's aggression against Ukraine and argue at least for U.S. isolationism if not for a change of sides in support of Russia.

Be aware that information warfare is the leading bow wave felt in advance of kinetic action. It is like those first few microseconds when a meteor enters the earth's atmosphere. There is a brief interval where resistance is gently felt – a gentle nudge and a little wisp of air. The pressure does not stop; instead influence ramps up exponentially, interval by interval, until the meteor is on fire and fragmenting into thousands of pieces.

Information warfare is ruthless; circumvention efforts must be similarly ruthless.

Authoritarians manipulate thinking in more ways than censoring the media and flooding it with counter narratives. They attack media platforms or technologies on which media platforms depend. Consider examples of Twitter and Alibaba.

Twitter was bought and gutted by Elon Musk. Musk is a super billionaire, originally from South Africa, and known to have right wing ideology. Twitter had been a leading social media platform, used by people across the spectrum of ideologies, languages, and education levels. Just about anyone who had something to say to the public or any company with a product to sell was posting short "tweets" on the platform.

As a corporate entity, owned by shareholders, Twitter had a responsibility to follow applicable laws against obscene content and a perogative to reject offensive content or hate speech. Upon completing his purchase of Twitter, Musk immediately overturned suspensions of far right accounts which had been kicked off due to hate speech, spamming and trolling, or disinformational postings. Fascist and hateful content surged on Twitter and appears to now be a permanent trait of the platform.

Jack Ma, the billionaire founder of Alibaba, disappeared from public view in 2020 amid signs of a power struggle between himself and the China Communist Party (CCP). Companies under the Alibaba umbrella do regulate their content and behavior according to industry regulations in China, which are strict. The party appears to have taken action against Ma after he gave a speech which contained wording openly critical of CCP policies. On October 24, during the Bund Summit, Ma argued that Chinese banking rules were outdated and needed to change. Soon afterward, he disappeared for more than two months, reappearing sporadically, but keeping a low profile. Ma makes no waves, lest he disappear permanently.

For saying the wrong words in a summit of globally influential economic and political figures, Ma was taken into custody. There was no public announcement of criminal or civil charges, no trial, and no transparency in the process of administering a penalty. Know for certain that in the future, no executive of Alibaba was going to stand up in public and judge government policies or regulations.

Before continuing to the next chapter, review the concept of information warfare. Nations, whether delimited by boundaries on a map or by lines of ethnicity and culture, have narratives about their origins and existence. Communication between people happens in an information environment, which is subject to biases one way or another.

Authoritarian or autocratic nations will use a broad rule set to guide censorship. The most aggressive ones will also use deliberate and malicious disinformation, especially where censorship will not work. Such actions by one nation against another is characterized as information warfare.

Circumventionism is a conscious and deliberate movement against information warfare. Because of the ruthlessness and scope of information warfare, circumventionist people must be equally if not more ruthless in resistance. Information has no borders and wants to be free; the same must be true of circumventionism.

# Chapter 4: Arrival of the Splinternet

Like the first blades of green grass breaking ground in the springtime, the internet arrived with great expectations. It was going to be everywhere. Every day, smart people were conceiving of new things which could be done if information could be managed in software and moved between computers, globally, within a split second.

A statement which was said before is so important that it bears repeating: information wants to be free. Going a little deeper, know that information is thermodynamic, much like heat and time:

- information disburses
- things seen cannot be unseen
- things heard cannot be unheard
- truths will eventually be discovered
- untruths are possible too

Obvious examples are easy to cite in scientific fields. Sooner or later, observers were bound to deduce that our solar system is centered on the sun. It was only a matter of time until the Calculus was discovered; Newton and Leibniz actually discovered it independently. Ditto for things we now know about biology and genetics. Because untrue information may exist, you should have a process for testing and vetting ideas to discover what is true.

Dictators deeply dislike the idea of democratized information and have been fighting it since the World Wide Web's early days. While autocrats are moderately effective at policing print, film, and broadcast media, an open internet is deadly poisonous to myths upon which dictatorships depend.

Think about the time when movable type, durable paper, and screw-driven presses were combined to make book reproduction so much faster and easier than copying by hand. Computers can reproduce, store, and transport not only words, but also images, sounds, and computing tools at a volume "orders of orders of magnitude" more than when the printing press was invented. Networks connect computers and the internet connects networks on a global scale. It is a nightmarish proposition for any autocrat to try and control modern information flows.

A two-pronged blacklist approach is how online censorship is typically implemented: force services to remove banned content and force internet access providers to block banned web domains.

In simplified terms, critical operations in a blacklist system are defining what data is to be removed, scanning for it, and then deleting banned data out of the system. To the average computer user, things mostly work, except that certain sites cannot be visited and certain items of content (phrases, images, files, or web links) cannot be shared.

Designers of computer censorship systems (and circumventionists who defeat them) understand the struggle to be powered by mathematics and electricity. Censors want to see everything which is passing through the network in order to find and remove banned content. They use *deep packet inspection* to read the data moving between clients and internet servers, then screen it for matches against prohibited content. Guess what can blind the censors so that they cannot tell what is passing through their filters? Encryption. Encryption breaks blacklist based censorship.

It is time for another important definition. Encryption is the process of converting plain language information, called cleartext, into a form, called cyphertext, which is unreadable. Decryption is the process of converting cyphertext back into the original cleartext information.

Some early forms of cryptography simply *transposed* all of the letters and numbers in a message to create cyphertext. Others used *substitution* of the letters and numbers. Mathematicians not only found ways to break all of the basic cyphers, but also discovered how to make new ones which are extremely difficult to break.

```
1    Cleartext:
2
3    Donald Trump is why my family
4    no longer likes mushrooms on
5    their pizza.
6
7
8    Cyphertext:
9
10   W8BeP256jbbb6ykOh0eR+FgE0gny/FkwILZN
11   HzzEigt+YtfcrdibRdLU1EhEJLN+NX3GMoPB
12   73UJWu9rkKcB5G9c8fafry4VhlUZyqG/5ab9
13   FNO796SF1adfbF6oV5zs
14
15
```

In public-key cryptosystems, the key for encryption may be made public, while a complementary private key is used for decryption. Keys may be arbitrarily powerful, such that a brute force crack could take billions of years.

Defeating censors who use blacklists is most often accomplished by using encryption to obscure clients' data, making it impossible to match with any blacklist. Obviously, it is possible to encrypt regular text in email or messages. Binary files such as images, music, or other documents may also be shared in encrypted form.

Accessing blacklisted websites is accomplished by using encrypted Domain Name Servers (DNS), proxies, or Virtual Private Networks (VPNs).

DNS is the first layer of censorship in most regimes. Computer users know their web domains by plain language names, such as "Twitter.com" or "NPR.org." Finding the corresponding internet protocol address for those canonical names is what DNS does. Censors block the process for blacklisted domains.

Proxies are web servers which act as intermediaries, useful for relaying traffic to and from blocked websites. They are a simple and low bandwidth solution to censorship for users who mostly want to read blogs or use basic social media.

An important aspect of proxying a connection is that an observer at the client's internet service provider sees the client connecting to an internet address not on the blacklist. Likewise, the website, which is still blacklisted, sees a connection coming from the proxy's address. Encryption at the proxy site is typically the Transport Layer Security (TLS) used to protect any "https" resource.

VPNs also change the IP address seen by an observer watching a client's connection or tracking connections at the remote website. VPNs offer vastly higher bandwidth than proxies and use more powerful encryption.

Of course, censors eventually became aware that their measures were being circumvented. Their response was to use better techniques to find proxies and VPNs. One important technique was to put more nodes on the net and observe traffic flows, seeking to find undiscovered VPNs and proxies. Another method, still popular, was to deploy teams of people (or automated bots) as subscribers to services, then compile lists of servers to blacklist.

China, employing leaders in the field of censorship, developed technology which not only searches data packets for contraband, but can evaluate connections and determine which type of VPN or proxy may be in use. Elements of the Great Firewall (GFW) are capable of actively probing the servers a client visits, testing it to verify whether it is being used for circumvention or not. Not only does the GFW use a DNS blacklist, it also sends "reset packets" to the client, causing it to stop loading the blocked page.

Privacy and anonymity are issues deeply intertwined with this topic of censorship versus circumvention. Censorship requires a lack of privacy, as the censor must know what a person is attempting to express or access through the network. Modern internet providers use deep packet inspection to see what we all read and write on the internet. You may feel that you have nothing to hide. That may be true today, but you may not feel so open when you need to discuss a serious health or family problem. Let us go for a ride on a crowded bus and talk aloud about your kidneys, a family member's death or another's divorce. Some information is truly private: only for people with a need to know.

Knowledge of our interests is mostly used for advertising algorithms. In a free country, a few specific wrong interests could be caught by the keyword screens and result in a user attracting law enforcement scrutiny. In a non-free country, a broad range of wrong interests could land a person on a police watch list, or result in an interview with authorities over a cup of tea.

Basic encryption provided by VPNs and proxies offers a measure of privacy. Perhaps the weakest privacy is through proxies, as TLS is not as strong as the encryption on VPNs. Anonymity, the trait of being an unknown user, is much more difficult to secure, thanks to the many methods attackers may use to uncloak a user. Always know that privacy is not the same thing as anonymity, and the risks of losing one are not the same as losing the other.

Consider what would be the next phase of competition between censorship regimes and circumventionists. More VPNs and Proxies, changing addresses frequently? Yes, in some cases. What other solution could there be? Congratulate yourself if you thought about *chaining a sequence of VPNs or proxies* so that the entry and exit addresses do not match! Chaining the connections increases the mathematical complexity of cracking either the privacy or anonymity of the network client.

"Tor" is an acronym for "The Onion Router." It is a project which provides anonymity to users by acting as a triple hop VPN hidden amid a vast population of possible relays.

Data from the client is sent to the first, or "guard" relay with three layers of encryption. The outer layer is decrypted and the data is forwarded to a middle relay. The second layer is decrypted and then data is sent to an exit node, where the inner layer is decrypted, revealing the original client data packets to be sent onward through the internet. Likewise, replies from the distant, uncensored service are sent back to the client through the reverse three hop onion routing.

Not only is the encryption for each layer sufficiently strong as to be impractical to attempt breaking, but the number of possible relays makes attempts to trace the connection impractically complex.

Tor enables millions of internet users to enjoy global connectivity with anonymity. It also enables sites to be set up which can be accessed from anywhere, no matter what censorship is enacted, save for a total network shutdown.

Global network connectivity is an asset to censorship circumvention, highlighting a weakness in the use of blacklists. All one needs to evade a blacklist is a foreign intermediary not on the list. When a VPN or proxy IP address is blacklisted, operators simply obtain a new address – a task which takes mere minutes.

Sooner or later, autocracies were bound to completely reject the global internet. What were they to do, with so many overseas VPNs and the Tor network available to internet users? One option was to "pull the plug" or shut down the internet, which inhibits commerce, stifles technological progress, and angers the citizens. Another option was to create a national intranet, which allows domestic connections (and effective censorship) but restrict access to foreign servers. Consider it to be a "greylisting" of all foreign internet resources, where all data packets would be inspected and rate limited at the national border.

When numerous countries set up cyber barriers against global internet connectivity, the phenomenon is known as *balkanization*. Iran, Russia, and China are the first countries which come to mind, but it has happened in more than thirty-five countries as of early 2023. If a time comes when the majority of countries balkanize their networks, the global internet will be lost, having degenerated into a *splinternet*.

When challenged as to why autocracies have shunned the global internet, officials offer a standard set of talking points mostly focused on fighting cyber crime or blocking obscene content. Make a list of their allies and run a matching algorithm on their talking points to see that they are primarily allies of Iran, Russia, and China. None of them ever admit the real reason for balkanizing their networks: protecting the official narrative which keeps their national leadership in power.

Reports of Russia's moves toward the splinternet appeared sporadically in media, dating from early 2019. Official talking points focused on hardening Russian infrastructure against cyber attacks and protecting data from hackers and cyber criminals. Consideration of the actual preparations, however, shows a fairly open network morphing into something more like the Chinese model. Russia was implementing censorship of their *domain name system* (DNS) and also requiring user data to be stored on servers within Russia – accessible by Russian law enforcement.

To use a polite euphemism, things "hit the fan" on March 4th,

2022. People in Russia who were using Twitter had noticed slow connection speeds. It was difficult and slow to get connected. Connectivity worsened throughout the day and Twitter gradually became inaccessible in Russia. Blocking Twitter was merely the beginning; a fully hardened national intranet blocks thousands of addresses. Things censored within the borders are blocked outside the borders. Social media, newspapers, archives and wikis, radio and television streamers, forums and blogs are all targets for blockage by the splinternet.

Splinternets provide a strongly coercive form of economic protectionism, keeping money flow directed toward businesses within the countries' borders. If you are within a splintered country, your choices of services to use are deliberately limited, without your consent. If you are a content creator or offer services on a major platform, you will lose visitors or customers due to cyber balkanization. You can have a million subscribers to a YouTube cooking channel but still be cut off from hundreds of millions of people who will never, ever, see any of your work.

When Twitter was blocked in Russia, people were offered a homegrown alternative: Vkontakte (VK). As a domestic service, VK maintains its hardware, software, and employees fully within jurisdiction of the Russian Federation. In China, like Russia, there are domestic alternatives for all of the major foreign computer services. Instead of Facebook, there is WeChat. Instead of Gmail, there is QQ. The situation is similar in any countries of the splinternet.

In some instances, online services operating within a country's intranet actually offer services at a quality and price desirable by their users. WeChat, for example, gets positive reviews, as it bundles a lot of useful services together. Other services only get customers because choices within a country are so limited. Other services, such as the BBC, New York Times, or the Internet Archive have no substitute. Remember, the splinternet is not an optional version of the internet; it is a compulsory censorship framework imposed on all network users within a country's jurisdiction.

How does a country enforce usage of its national intranet? What stops everyone from immediately finding ways to evade the censorship? It is a matter of technical measures, gentle nudges, and hard coercion.

As mentioned earlier, foreign web domains found to offer banned content are blocked. Such content could be news or tabloid coverage which contradicts the official narrative. It could be content which is embarrassing to members of the ruling class or governing party. It could be anything, subject to the whims and prejudices of whomever has the power to censor.

Since VPNs, proxies, and Tor are tools used to circumvent network censorship, they are highly restricted. It may be surprising, but even in the People's Republic of China, there are domestic VPNs used to secure networking on public wifi – in coffee shops and other places, or for networking within businesses. Foreign VPN servers and Tor are detected, checked, and blocked by the Great Firewall.

Secure web pages, which use TLS encryption and have the "https" prefix are restricted in some countries. Kazakhstan, for example, has been trying to force computer users to install a fake *root certificate* in their web browser software. The certificate would allow government surveillance of the user's browsing and was found to have been used to intercept data from top search engines, language translators, email, and social media.

TLS encryption serves two protective functions: preventing surveillance from third parties and assuring authenticity of the data transferred. It means that when you visit a TLS encrypted page, your network provider cannot inspect your packets and see what you are doing or steal your data. It also means no intermediary can make changes to the data while it is enroute. If the TLS is compromised by a forced government root certificate, it can no longer be trusted.

Another aspect of secure web browsing is the matter of Encrypted Server Name Indication (ESNI), recently renamed to Encrypted

Client Hello (ECH). What it does is verify and encrypt the website domain name being visited and assure that the proper website TLS certificate is used. When ECH is used, censors cannot watch the TLS data and learn which website is being visited. Russia and the PRC are both known to block ECH.

Forced usage of fake root certificates is not simply a matter of excessively broad government surveillance; it opens a back door which could be exploited by criminals. All it takes is a successful hack of the government's computers where the keys are stored, and criminals would have what they need to hack users' browsing sessions.

Another technical measure countries use to keep their people separated from the global internet is to restrict available operating systems used on computing devices and then to restrict which applications may be installed. Indeed, Microsoft's Windows and Apple's macOS are available, popular and packed with useful apps as elsewhere. Except... Within splinternets, apps associated with banned websites are unavailable. Facebook, Twitter, Dropbox, and Gmail, for example, are unavailable in China.

Android is highly popular on the many models of smartphones and tablets people use on a daily basis. Each manufacturer tends to use their own special version of Android, with branding, performance tweaks, or other features. One feature which is not so friendly or convenient is censored DNS...

Censorship and surveillance experts in earlier years have cited restrictions built into state sponsored operating systems, such as North Korea's *Red Star OS*. The same may seem to apply to China's *HarmonyOS*. Looking more closely, HarmonyOS is more of a marketing idea, in which it runs on a huge number of different pricey devices Huawei hopes to sell. Censorship is baked in to the extent that regulations require system apps to monitor media on a device and report or block banned content. Free countries are welcoming such monitoring for the Apple and Google ecosystems.

Don't fall into a false sense of security that a device from South

Korea or Japan cannot have a compromised operating system, for three reasons:

- Phones for sale in a specific country may be required to contain surveillance apps or be configured for censored DNS.

- Any users could do something to get the attention of police or intelligence services and be targeted for surveillance apps.

- Hackers and ransomware groups are constantly deploying their tools, which will infect devices of anyone who is not careful enough (or simply unlucky).

At least a few people in any country on the splinternet will be interested in defeating the censorship, referred to as "jumping the wall." With the best circumvention methods, the local network provider and its government partners will not know that their restrictions have been overcome. Older or less sophisticated circumvention methods may escape scrutiny if the number of users is small or the amount of data involved isn't significant.

The PRC is probably the most prolific censoring country, with the GFW requiring more effort to beat than most people are willing to expend. There are some people, though, who will jump the wall and transfer many gigabytes of data – downloading movies, music, images, books, or whatever is of interest. Reports indicate that when the authorities decide to get involved, they gradually escalate pressure as necessary to stop the person from circumventing censorship.

The first penalty is generally a restriction on the person's internet, which may be an automatic step carried out by the internet provider. Next, the person may be visited by police officers who may issue a warning or give an "invitation to have a talk over some tea" at the police station. Creating, sharing, or selling VPNs or other circumvention services is a serious matter - enough for a person to be arrested.

Masha Borak, of the *South China Morning Post* reported in July of 2020 about the case of a man in the PRC named Chen, who was punished for using a VPN to access adult entertainment sites on the global internet. Chen was located in Jinshi, Hunan province, where he was using an application called *Shadowrocket* to jump over the wall and find some arousing videos. For using a VPN not registered with the government and downloading prohibited material, Chen faced a fine of RMB 15000, which amounted to a little over USD $2100 at the time.

Sarah Zheng reported, in a 2017 article in the *'Post* that Wu Xiangyang, from the Guangxi Zhuang region, had been busted for selling unregistered VPN services. Wu was sentenced to 5½ years in prison and fined RMB 500,000 (USD $76000).

In the 2022 *World Press Freedom Index*, published by Reporters Without Borders (RSF), Iran ranks 178th out of 180 countries – where only Eritrea and North Korea are worse. People in Iran are like other people. They want to have access to media, to know what is going on, and to be able to engage for discussion about issues of daily life. Outside of Iran, there is a pretty active diaspora on social media, active at any hour of the day on topics such as education, jobs, history, food, Iranian culture, and even tourism.

Instagram and WhatsApp were blocked in late September 2022 amid unrest over the death of Mahsa Amini. Amini, age 22, died while in police detention, arrested under accusation of improperly wearing her hijab. As authorities increased their death grip on the network, demand for VPNs increased by a factor of **thirty**. People are very willing to defy authority to be in touch with the outside world and are exposing themselves to the associated risks – at least until the religious extremists running Iran are *dealt with*.

When autocracies lose the ability to effectively censor and control their national networks, they *shut them down*. As an advocate for people using VPNs and other circumvention tools to access the global internet from restrictive environments, I have often asserted that the tools "work until authorities pull the plug and disconnect." Recent history shows that internet shutdowns are happening, at increasing rates. Frankly, the problem is not technical, but is instead a problem of too many authoritarians being allowed to run and ruin countries.

If you have not done it already, drop the belief that billionaires and strongmen are the best people to run countries. They loot national coffers, destroy vital institutions, and fill the media with myths, such as "I'll make the trains run on time."

Internet shutdowns amount to collective restraint and mistreatment across regions and whole countries. Shutdowns are

# Reasons for Internet Shutdowns

Protests
Examinations
Elections
Warfare
Genocides / Massacres

economically harmful, preventing businesses from operating and doing their part to provide jobs and help people put food on their tables. In areas of unrest or natural disaster, shutdowns prevent aid workers, journalists, and observers from doing their jobs. Shutdowns are ostensibly used to prevent cheating during school exams such as China's gaokao and numerous exams in India.

India has been the leading country conducting internet shutdowns for the most recent 5 years ending in 2022. Access Now, in their recent report, *Internet Shutdowns in 2022*, states that internet service was deliberately cut off in 35 countries. It is a trend which has been increasing since 2017, with India far out ahead of all others. The reasons appear to be vague and impulsive, without due consideration of the effects or weighed against alternative remedies.

Numerous other countries use intentional internet shutdowns to serve their purposes. All are to impede communication of groups considered to be adversaries: students, political opposition, protesters, and other marginalized people.

In the next chapter, we will discuss tools for destruction of splinternets and finding your favorite radio show on the other side of the world.

# Chapter 5: Tools for Circumvention

Forty-eight countries have severely restricted media and / or personal expression. Seventy-two percent of people today are living in autocracies, amounting to 5,779,146,132 persons if I run a quick calculation using Worldometers' estimate of population at the minute of this writing. That is a *lot* of persons with reasons to not speak freely to their friends and acquaintances. How many of them have a sense that they are being lied to about important aspects of daily life? I assert that there exists a huge interest in ways to say what is real and to hear it from others.

Censorship and disinformation, at the level of nation-states, may appear to be immense, unscalable obstacles, but know this: all barriers are permeable. Appearance of solidity is among the biggest myths of censorship regimes, a vapor awaiting dispersal when hit by a wind at the proper angle. The principal weakness of internet censorship infrastructure is rigidity: targeting in such a specific way that they fail to block content which is sufficiently different from things in the blacklist. As pointed out in the previous chapter, encrypting data is often enough. Another way censorship systems fail is when people simply refuse to use the expected platforms and instead find alternate ways to reach freedom.

Censorship and its circumvention is an arms race, requiring attention and action. For every system used by autocrats to control the media and muzzle expression, people find ways to beat it. Then the circumvention gets blocked, forcing opponents to exploit a different weakness in the system. If you are a user of circumvention tools, be prepared to get updates from time to time. If you are an aspiring creator or developer, never, ever stop learning about your opponent, where his systems have flaws to exploit, and what you should do to hollow out his ability to wage information warfare.

Two systematic ways to think about censorship circumvention can be borrowed from other endeavors. Look these up on the web or in a good library. First is SWOT analysis. The acronym stands for "Strengths, Weaknesses, Opportunities, and Threats" and it directs thought towards understanding what a system does well, not so well, where it could find new ways to work, and how it could be broken. The other systematic process is running "OODA" loops, meaning to "Observe - Orient - Decide - Act" repeatedly. In practical terms, you have a tool set of actions to take in handle the censors. Before acting, you must observe what is happening, figure out the context or what the observations mean, select the proper tool to handle the problem, and finally doing something. After doing something, the cycle is repeated.

Circumvention tools in this chapter are software tools you may download, install, and use. Do not worry too much about your computer or phone's operating system. The best tools are available on Windows, macOS, many flavors of Linux, and the BSDs. Another aspect to consider is which operating system is most resistant to attacks by malware and spyware - tools often used in autocracies to monitor computer users, steal data, and sometimes destroy data. Windows tends to be targeted more than the others; Linux and BSD systems the least, with macOS in the middle. No matter which system is on your computing devices use, it is very necessary to use a good scanner and keep your devices clean. Learn the habits of safe computing to stay free and avoid harm.

I make a pitch here for Linux, for it is a system which embraces freedom and open software, may be customized and shared easily as a complete system, and works on all sorts of devices - phones, tablets, laptops, and servers. Some may be written to a USB flash drive and booted up to run on a personal computer without actually modifying it. Shutdown and unplug the USB drive and no one would know that a different system had been running minutes before.

Consider these Linux systems for ready-made computing with included privacy and anti-censorship software:

- Qubes - run applications in protected environments and with Tor or VPNs

- Whonix - oriented around comprehensive anonymity, privacy, and security

- Tails - hardened Linux focused on privacy and anonymity

- MOFO Linux - Multimedia, streaming radio, VPNs proxies, and Tor

The systems above are all effective and useful platforms, set up with circumvention tools which can break out of any of the worlds's splinternets for access to the global internet. A description of several types of tools will now be discussed.

## Encrypted Domain Name Servers (DNS)

One of the first things censoring countries do is apply a DNS blacklist for domain names and IP addresses. Blocked domains are either blocked or redirected to something else, such as a fake Facebook or fake Twitter.

Censoring countries have recently started blocking DNS-over-TLS (DoT), as it uses a unique port for its queries. Good news is that DNS-over-HTTPS (DoH) continues to work, using standard port 443, and it is unlikely to be blocked. To block DoH would also block all secure web pages, which experts believe to be too broadly disruptive. DoH may be set up in Firefox and other web browsers.

Attacks on DNS can be thwarted by forwarding queries through circumvention tools to reliable servers. Also, DNS may not be necessary when using Tor *hidden services* or other *overlay* networks.

## Proxies

The most basic and simple network censorship circumvention tool is the proxy server. Its purpose is to provide an IP address and domain name, not on any blacklist, for relaying the requests and responses between a client and an otherwise blocked website.

Proxies tend to be small resources set up on a server, much like a website, but with code written to connect visitors to other web pages. Users can work through a proxy by visiting the proxy in their web browser, then entering the blocked site URL into a text field. Upon execution, the blacklisted site is unblocked and works. It is also possible to use a proxy without visiting an intermediate page by globbing the two URLs. For example, to visit radio free Asia, the glob could look like this:

```
https://example-proxy.com:8000/https://www.rfa.org/english/
```

In the example above, the proxy service has the domain name "example-proxy.com" and takes proxying requests on port 8000. The proxy URL is separated from the desired endpoint with a simple forward slash, but syntax can vary from one proxy site to another.

Web browsers can be configured, in their connection settings, to use proxies in a more transparent fashion. Usually, the configuration is a matter of checking a box to enable proxying, then entering the proxy IP address and port number. After that, proxying is transparent, requiring no further intervention from the user. Just enter an address and it gets proxied.

On my Linux system, I have an application called *Proxychains*. It works at a deeper level than the web browser, and when running, intercepts the browser's traffic and routes it through one, two, three, or any number of proxies in a chain. Such a connection would be extremely difficult for an observer to track from end to end. As a practical matter, a chain of three proxies worked alright for reading pages of text, but were not usable for pages with large images, video, or audio.

Security can vary on proxy servers. The oldest ones were deployed decades ago and did not use SSL or TLS encryption. Nor were they safe to use to view secure HTTPS websites. Newer proxies do use TLS; *squid* and *socks* proxy types work safely with TLS protected websites.

Proxies will work until the authorities find and blacklist them. If you go online looking for proxy lists, you will see that most are listed as IP addresses rather than domain names. Domains are expensive to buy and register in massive numbers; IPs are not.

## Shadowsocks

Working in a manner between proxies and VPNs, Shadowsocks was invented by an anonymous Chinese programmer who posted his code on GitHub under the username of "Clownwindy." He saw that socks proxies were fast, but needed a strong encryption to protect users' privacy, especially in non-free countries like the PRC.

PRC authorities took a keen interest in Shadowsocks because it was so effective against their censorship system and had become very widely used. To stop the spread of Shadowsocks, GitHub was blacklisted. Reports indicated that the software site became slower and slower, until it became inaccessible. Chinese software developers and system admins complained that they couldn't do their jobs due to the blockage. Fairly quickly, authorities relented and unblocked GitHub.

Police found Clownwindy. At first, they asked him to stop working on Shadowsocks. A couple of days later, they returned with a demand that he completely delete the code he had written and maintained. Fortunately, Shadowsocks had been cloned by others who wanted to work on it themselves, and it continues to exist today. A handful of varieties exist, all working to unblock the internet for millions of people around the world.

## Virtual Private Networks (VPNs)

VPNs enable a network user to enjoy the experience of connecting as though in another location. To experience the internet as though in the United Kingdom, use a VPN server in London or Liverpool. To experience the internet as though in Japan, use a VPN server in Osaka or Tokyo. When connecting to the various services on the internet, they recognize the client location as being at the VPN server.

A VPN provides privacy between their computer and the VPN server, with a strongly encrypted link between the two. Deep packet inspection at the client's service provider will find randomized, noise-like data. The experience is transparent in that web browsing, streaming, or any other activity "just works" as though the person was located at the server. On the client computer, applications connecting to the internet will interact with a virtual tunnel interface, which passes data to and from the VPN's encryption and formatting package. It is encrypted VPN data which passes through the computer's wireless or ethernet hardware. At the distant end of a VPN connection, data is decrypted and then sent onward through the network to its final destination.

If the original data was encrypted before going into the VPN, as when visiting a TLS protected web page, it comes out of the VPN wrapped in that original encryption. It is as though you are wearing a red sweater and temporarily put on a huge woolen trench coat and go for a walk outside in cold weather. When you step indoors and remove your coat, the red sweater is still there.

OpenVPN, Wireguard, and SoftEther are currently the top VPN types. All three provide great security, especially when large keys are used. An older type, loved by ratty, aging corporate systems is Level Two Tunneling Protocol (L2TP). It is possibly compromised and should be avoided. Wireguard has an advantage over the others. It is very well designed, fast, and secure. All VPN types are targeted for blocking by the censoring countries, except they do not appear to be very successful against Wireguard.

Attacks against VPNs consist of finding *fingerprints* - recognizable patterns in sequences of data - which reveal the type of encryption in use by a VPN. China's GFW has an active probing system which observes users' connections and tests suspicious servers to look for a VPN-like response. A suspicious connection is one with little readable text and lots of random characters. If active probing reveals a VPN server, it is added to the national blocklist.

Philipp Winter gave a stunning lecture before the Chaos Communication Congress in 2015, for a research paper he and several colleagues published, titled *Examining How the Great Firewall Discovers Hidden Circumvention Servers*. He made it very clear how sophisticated the acting probing system is. It appears to have a large number of specialized modules which match fingerprints for VPNs and other anti-censorship systems. In the year 2012, the system would build a target list and respond with probes in regular fifteen minute intervals. By the time of Winter's talk at 32C3, the prober had been upgraded to work in real-time, contacting its targets within 500 milliseconds.

Because servers are blocked so quickly, the best VPNs must offer a large number of servers, change IP addresses regularly, and work with good obfuscation methods.

Trustworthiness is an important factor in selecting a VPN service. A VPN provider which keeps logs of client activity (times and IP addresses) may be required to give user data to law enforcement if demanded. There are numerous cases of political activists being tracked, arrested, and imprisoned thanks to dictators obtaining VPN logs. If you pick a commercial VPN service, make sure they do not keep logs. A better solution is to have your own server abroad, with a VPN installed, and configure it to not keep logs.

Decentralized VPNs are a new and promising phenomenon. They operate as a "zero trust" service, where the user does not need to trust the server operators in any way and operators know nothing about the users. The operating principle is somewhat like *onion routing*, with the client's data being encrypted, divided, and routed through multiple servers before being sent out to the global internet.

## Secure Shell (SSH)

Secure shell is a usable circumvention tool which can often escape being blocked by censorship regimes. SSH is how webmasters and server administrators connect to machines in data centers for maintenance tasks. Some people have servers set up as "remote desktop" systems to do all the things we all do with our personal computers, except the remote system is somewhere far away. As a maintenance or administration tool, SSH is considered to be necessary and non-threatening. When dictators intensify their attacks on internet connectivity, SSH is the *last* service to be taken down.

Most people think of SSH as just a terminal window or command prompt connected to a distant computer. Circumventionists think of SSH an encrypted connection with fairly high bandwidth, which can evade censorship with less probability of being blocked. Using SSH transparently, just like a VPN, is simply a matter of translating the various addresses and ports for applications to the distant server.

SSH may be set up to function VPN-like by using an application like *Sshuttle*. It may also be done by manually entering commands in the computer's terminal emulator. It is my opinion that SSH is an essential tool for people in the worst autocracies. Servers with SSH access are cheap and plentiful all over the world.

## The Onion Router (Tor)

When the consequences of using a compromised VPN are unacceptable, can a person use something stronger? It is a problem involving risks other than the encryption being cracked, revealing content being passed through the VPN by a client. There may be danger associated with an attacker getting user logs and determining the times a certain client is on the VPN or discovering which IP addresses are involved.

Just imagine the potential risks to women in American states like Texas or South Carolina, if legislatures successfully prohibit accessing websites giving information on contraception or abortion, if the banned information is accessed. Consider the risks of publishing critical political speech in Florida, where the thirteen year-old son of activist and whistle-blower Rebekah Jones was arrested for posting memes in a private chat.

Muhammad Bilal Khan was a Pakistani micro blogger who posted a lot of content about contentious topics related to Islam. He also drew attention to forced disappearances which were happening, with suspicions focused on the military and police. In June of 2019, at age 22, Khan was killed after being set up as prey for a mob of angry, knife wielding men. The only reason anyone could get to him was because his Twitter account was not anonymous.

Stakes are high for as many varied reasons as there are people. Even private individuals who are *not* public figures may have a need for strong privacy and anonymity, strong enough to resist *any* attack, with *no exceptions at all*. Mathematics provides an answer to the question of how to make a system robust enough to use with *zero trust*. In other words, what kind of internet privacy and anonymity system can circumvent censorship, not reveal information about the users, and not reveal information about the content of the communications - even if the system is attacked by nation-states?

Onion routing is the answer. It has been referenced in another section of this book, but it warrants explanation here. These are critically important features which distinguish Tor:

- zero trust – works if one server is compromised
- multiple hop routing for anonymity
- multiple encryption layers for privacy
- supports hidden services
- more resistant than VPNs to timing or analysis attacks
- software well vetted and open source
- may be concealed with pluggable transports

Data packets sent to a Tor entry node are protected by an outer layer of encryption, with two more layers beneath that, protecting the original data from client applications (web browsing, file transfers, media streaming, etc). Leaving the entry node, data has two remaining layers of encryption and goes to an intermediate node. The intermediate node peels off another layer of encryption and relays the packets to an exit node. At the exit node, the last layer of Tor encryption is peeled off and the client's original data packets are sent onward through the global internet.

Hidden services, called *onion sites*, may operate within Tor itself. They offer two way privacy and anonymity, such that visitors and sites may interact while not knowing the other's identity.

An attacker attempting to track a user through the network has an incredibly difficult problem. There are more than 6000 Tor nodes operating at this time, with about four million users. It may not initially seem to be a complex problem, but millions of users connecting to thousands of entry points connecting to thousands of intermediaries connecting to thousands of exit nodes amounts to a problem too large to solve within a reasonable period of time. It is simply not practical, with any number of computers, to check all the possible combinations of servers. Tor's anonymity strength is in hiding users within a very large crowd.

Setting up and simultaneously controlling hundreds of guard, exit, and relay nodes is known as a *Sybil* attack. From the guard node, the attacker learns who is connecting; from the exit node, the attacker learns what the client is doing. Sybil attacks not work for deanonymizing *specific* users on demand, as the client's Tor software has a low probability of selecting all three nodes which are controlled by the attacker.

Another way to attack the anonymity feature of Tor is to attempt to find timing correlations as traffic passes through the network. Doing so requires control of a large number of guard and exit nodes. When an attacker can match time and size patterns for traffic entering Tor with traffic leaving Tor, the user can be deanonymized.

Without deanonymizing a user or cracking the encryption, access to Tor can be denied by obtaining IP addresses of Tor directory servers. China blocked a huge number of Tor nodes by finding the directory server list and blocking every one of the servers on it. In order to maintain Tor connectivity in places controlled by such a capable adversary, a separate group of unlisted servers, called *bridges* were made available on request.

*Pluggable Transports* are various small software modules which connect to bridges via clever encrypting proxies, obfuscating the Tor fingerprint. An important feature is separating "privacy" from "anonymity."

An observer will see traffic which looks different from Tor, routed to servers which do not appear to behave as Tor nodes. Several pluggable transports exist; new ones are being created and developed at any time. These are some of the nifty pluggable transport modules:

- Scramblesuit: modifies the network fingerprint and

protects against follow-on probing

- Obfs4: randomizes traffic so that it does not appear to be associated with Tor

- Meek: uses domain fronting under principle of *collateral freedom*

- FTE: format transforming encryptions such that traffic resembles a stream of unencrypted text

- Snowflake: small proxies running in web browsers, brokered on domain fronting servers

Pluggable transports using domain fronting are located on server IP addresses shared with important web services. Blocking those addresses would cause too much trouble, too much *collateral damage*. If the censoring regime does not block the domain, that domain provides *collateral freedom*!

Pluggable transports are also adaptable to circumvention tools other than Tor. A popular adaptation is usage of Obfs4 with either OpenVPN or Proxychains.

## Lokinet

Lokinet is a decentralized anonymity network with onion routing, operating as an overlay atop the global internet. Creators sought a system with strong privacy and anonymity, similar to Tor, but with a distributed directory and high resistance to Sybil attacks. What they created is known as low *latency anonymous routing protocol* and operates on the Oxen block chain.

Lokinet handles activities such as web browsing, using hidden services, file transfers, secure messaging, etc. Technically, it is more flexible than Tor.

What is Lokinet's main weakness? It has a much lower number of users than Tor, with far fewer hidden services. It is so tightly associated with Oxen blockchain and cryptocurrency that potential users perceive Lokinet as an internet toll road, with questionable value for the price.

## Invisible Internet Project (I2P)

I2P is a decentralized, fully encrypted, peer to peer network running as an overlay atop the global internet. It has some similarities but also some important differences with Tor. I2P is a much smaller network than Tor, with an estimated population of 55,000 users, plus or minus a few thousand. The network is far more decentralized, without directory servers as on Tor, but instead using a distributed database called the *netDb*. The network is self-contained, with almost all of its content on nodes within I2P much like Tor's hidden services. Very few connections to the public internet are available on I2P; it seeks to build forums, chats, file sharing and other interactivity within the network.

Traffic is moved in a unidirectional *garlic routing* scheme which features secure end-to-end encryption. This is a significant security improvement over onion routing, which is bidirectional and not end-to-end encrypted. I2P's unidirectional routing is more secure, as there is less for an attacker to learn about any clients on a node. What's more, I2P's end-to-end encrypted data gains the inherent benefit of authentication. Both users and the sites they interact with are anonymized.

As a peer to peer network, the users of I2P form the network itself; they function as *routers* and pass data through tunnels to other *routers*. Because of the multiple layers of encryption and one-way tunnels, it is extremely unlikely for an attacker with control of a router to learn enough about other users to deanonymize them.

As with Tor, adversaries may try to disrupt the network by conducting DDOS attacks. I2P appears to be more resistant to these attacks, as evidenced by migration of *Dread* forum users from Tor to I2P.

Now, a word about I2P clients. I2P has a widely used Java client which is overly large and inefficient. Use the vastly better *i2pd* client. I2pd is a daemon, written in C++, which has numerous and important advantages over the Java implementation. It is smaller, uses less computer resources, and is very fast. I2P works almost as fast as the public internet when using i2pd - fast enough for real time video meetings or streaming live radio programming.

How well does I2P work for its users? It is an active network with users producing and using all sorts of content. When first connecting, the user doesn't have much information about resources available, as there is no central directory or index. At least a couple of hours is needed before a significant amount of *netDb* data is received and a working network map is built. Then the user can successfully find forums, markets, libraries, or other resources. With the i2pd client, the experience is smooth and responsive.

## Project Geneva

Artificial intelligence (AI), when applied to persistent problems, can offer solutions which put an end to their persistence, making them *formerly existing* problems. Project Geneva is said to be an acronym for "genetic evasion" and uses AI against censorship. Not only does Geneva study the behavior of censors in order to find weaknesses, it acts smartly, deploying tricks and traps which cause censorship to fail. Geneva has done some interesting work against internet censorship systems running in India, China, and Kazakhstan.

Censorship systems can be classified as operating *in-path* or *on-path*. An in-path operation is an element which receives user data, checks it for contraband, and either passes it downstream, rewrites it to replace the contraband, or deletes the offending data. On-path operations monitor data passing through the network, without directly changing it, and take action to break a connection if contraband is detected. On-path censorship is less expensive and takes far less computing power than in-path censorship.

Surprisingly to myself, who has actually experienced censorship by China's GFW, most of its stopping power is exercised as on-path actions. It monitors DNS requests and does deep packet inspection on connections between clients and servers.

DNS requests for a prohibited web page are poisoned, meaning a bogus response is quickly sent to the client. If DNS poisoning fails and the browser contacts the distant server with a page request, the GFW on-path component will quickly send reset (RST) packets to kill the connection. It all takes a fraction of a second to happen and is successful as long as the RST packets get to the client before the real response from the distant server. What the user sees is a blank screen or perhaps a "Connection Reset" error message.

In their 2019 research paper, *Geneva: Evolving Censorship Evasion Strategies*, computer scientists Kevin Bock, George Hughey, Xiao Qiang, and Dave Levin reported how well Geneva's genetic algorithms work against actual censorship schemes. When unleashed, it would discover *species* of circumvention strategies, with *sub-species* and *variants* in a matter of mere hours.

In 27 experiments against China's GFW, Geneva discovered four species, eight sub-species, and twenty-one distinct sub-variants. Running against India and Kazakhstan, it discovered five species. In a laboratory environment, Geneva found thirty out of thirty-six strategies suggested by the prior work of experts. The authors believed the algorithm would have found more strategies if it had been allowed to act with a wider range of parameters.

With the help of artificial intelligence, circumventionists are bound to ream and make hollow the censorship systems which infringe on the freedoms of expression of so many people.

## Yggdrasil Network

Yggdrasil operates as an end-to-end encrypted mesh network overlaid on the global internet. It is a decentralized network, with routing information distributed throughout, and no central control or single points of failure. Clients on the network also function as routers, adding to Yggdrasil's robustness and ability to self-heal when nodes go offline.

At the time of this writing, there are about 5,183 Yggdrasil nodes running.

## Wireless Mesh Networks

During recent events of civil unrest in the Middle East, Asia, Africa, and Europe, local governments noticed that mobile internet service was being used for coordination by tech savvy protesters. When internet service was shut down in an attempt to hinder the coordination, protesters showed how tech savvy they really were. It was amusing to me how authorities, mostly of the Boomer generation, were taken by surprise when angry young people simply switched to applications which used short range *mesh networking* over bluetooth and wifi.

Conventional chat and messaging applications rely on a central server to either relay messages between users or hold them for retrieval. Interaction between participants is not possible if the central server is taken offline or if there is no network to access it. That is why authorities shut down the internet where civil unrest is happening. When protesters use mesh networking to communicate, they act independently of the public internet and are unaffected by shutdowns. Mesh networking smartphones apps form network nodes, passing messages directly to adjacent nodes and acting as relays along a route to more distant ones. Typical range for a smartphone mesh network is about 60 meters between wifi or bluetooth nodes; maximum network area is limited only by the number and positioning of more phones.

Mesh networks are not required to pass data in real time. It is common for apps to have a store-and-forward capability in which the device will retain data until it can make contact with another node and pass it onward. In other words, people who travel with mesh networked devices can transfer messages and files on a global scale.

**Firechat** is arguably the most famous mesh networking application. It is now discontinued, but it played a part in protests which happened in multiple countries during the middle 2010s. Hong Kong's *Umbrella Movement* protests happened during the summer and fall of 2014 amid undemocratic changes being made to the region's electoral system, under political pressure from Beijing. Young people took to the streets, protests grew in both size and loudness, and at the end of September, crowds so large that the cell towers were at maximum user capacity. As mobile data grew unreliable, protesters used Firechat to maintain contact and stay coordinated. There were over 100,000 downloads during a 24 hour period at the end of September.

Alex Hern, reporting for *The Guardian* in June, 2014, said that 40,000 people in Iraq had downloaded Firechat, making it the second biggest user in the world, behind Hong Kong and just ahead of Iran.

Firechat had a critical weakness, however. It lacked encryption, which was not added until mid-2015. Without encryption, users lacked privacy and could not authenticate messages. They were subject to surveillance and injection of fake messages into the chats.

**Serval Mesh** is another project of the middle 2010s, originating from Australia's Flinders University, seeking to provide mesh networking on smartphones. It emphasized robustness and independence from the terrestrial cellular networks. It was pitched as the communications app which still works when natural disasters strike. While it was in active development, I actually used it, finding that it worked well, setting up ad-hoc wifi meshes. For natural disaster response, the project did work on augmenting the mesh with wireless devices other than wifi. As of early 2023, the project appears to have stalled. It has gone several months with no updates to its online software repositories and no stable releases since June of 2016.

**Bridgefy** has a description on the company web page which is clear about its purpose, as a "free messaging app that works without the Internet. Perfect for natural disasters, large events, and at school!" It uses bluetooth communications to build a mesh network with other Bridgefy equipped phones. During the 2019-2020 time frame, there were record setting protests in Hong Kong and India, which put a strain on phone network infrastructure. In some instances, phone and mobile data services were intentionally disrupted by their governments. Bridgefy successfully helped people stay in contact.

Attacks against Bridgefy can teach important lessons about security and robustness of mesh networking applications if they are to be used during protests and shutdowns. The number one problem with versions of Bridgefy available in 2019 and 2020 was weak encryption, making messages readable by attackers as well as subject to spoofing. In the research paper, *Mesh Networking in Large-Scale Protests: Breaking Bridgefy*, University of London scientists highlighted the possibility that an attacker could read Bridgefy messages and create a database of users. With a database of users and lists of their contacts, which governments could compel from corporate service providers, authorities could derive user interrelationships.

Without a tamper-resistant means of authentication, an attacker could impersonate other users or send fake broadcast messages to groups. Not ony does that create a risk of disinformation, but also of cyber attacks on the application itself.

During the time of those protests in Hong Kong and India, Bridgefy sent messages in compressed format. A clever attack, known as *zip bombing* involves sending a highly compressed message which decompresses into an extremely large file. Zip bombing Bridgefy could cause it to crash.

Bridgefy developers updated the application in mid 2021, incorporating end-to-end encryption and stronger message authentication. Martin Albrecht, an author of the *Breaking Bridgefy* paper, joined with Raphael Eikenberg and Kenneth Paterson (of ETH Zurich's Applied Cryptography Group) to evaluate the new version's security. The new Bridgefy was more secure than the old, but not enough to prevent *motivated attackers* from capturing enough data to intercept messages, impersonating others in the broadcast channel, and sending zip bombs.

Governments and organized crime organizations are never anything less than motivated attackers. They will spend as much money and hire as many experts as necessary to conduct attacks or get data they want from messaging applications. You should always be a *motivated adversary* and use the strongest privacy and anonymity applications you can find.

## Wifi Meshes

One would expect, in 2023, for there to be plenty of wifi mesh networks in towns and cities around the world, as the hardware, software, and skill requirements are moderate at worst, and sometimes rather easy. Some do exist. They serve as great examples of how to make connectivity available to more people. It is entirely possible to host web services, forums, or other resources on servers connected to the local wifi mesh.

Good news is that the older wifi mesh networks, with temperamental routers, special firmware, and antenna kludges are giving way to equipment designed expressly to serve as mesh nodes. Wifi 6 makes deployment an uncomplicated matter.

Listed here are some of the interesting projects extending

network connectivity across communities. Enter these into your favorite search engine to learn details of the projects and discover more links to follow:

- Guifi (Spain)

- Freifunk (Germany)

- Coolab (Brazil)

- PYMESH (India)


Community wifi meshes are like other meshes: decentralized, with network nodes both carrying traffic for the net and also having knowledge of routing to other nodes. With nodes mounted on rooftops and streetlight poles, connectivity can reach indoor nodes mounted near windows. Certain super nodes also connect to the global internet through the area's internet provider. Even during times when the internet is shut down, community meshes can still operate if electrical power is available.

Slow adoption of community wifi mesh networks has a couple of large reasons, rooted in economics and security. Mobile phone service providers oppose community wireless nets, instead wanting to offer data services for profit to residents. They make mobile data ubiquitous and *affordable enough* for residents to subscribe.

As to the security issue, operators of mesh nodes do not want liability for the actions of visitors on their network. It is so much easier to hold network users accountable for what they do on their personal mobile data accounts. Of course, mobile data is a centralized service, subjecting clients to control and monitoring from the service provider's facilities.

## Secure Messaging Applications

Although not designed as mesh networking applications, four

messaging tools merit mentioning here, due to their strong security and decentralized infrastructure. All four are worthy of use by activists, journalists, or people subject to undue censorship and surveillance.

**Briar** offers "secure messaging, anywhere" and is available for Android devices. It uses peer-to-peer, end-to-end communication, passing text and emojis only. Users may contact others through direct messages or post to forums. If the recipient of a message is near, Briar may use bluetooth or wifi to send data; otherwise, it will pass traffic through Tor in order to have anonymity.

**Element** is a messenger built around the *Matrix* protocol and a federated structure, meaning that it uses a network of independent servers which may be linked together to serve a common set of users. No single party owns a person's messages. Traffic moves in a distributed manner, over all participants. Encryption is end-to-end.

Element is envisioned as an application suitable for individuals, groups, and large companies. It is capable of handling text, files, video or audio, sent either as direct messages or group chats. I have used Element for a couple of years and am quite satisfied with how it works.

**Session** originated as a fork of the *Signal* private messenger and has developed into a magnificent application in its own right. It uses end-to-end encryption, a resilient peer-to-peer network structure for security, plus onion routing for anonymity. Note that Session's onion routing is provided by the same Oxen nodes used by Lokinet.

One of the most notable things differentiating Session from Signal is that it does not require a user's phone number. Session, instead, generates a special alphanumeric Session ID for account management.

Session is versatile, capable of passing messages of text, images, audio, and small files.

**White Mouse** gets its name from the nickname of Nancy Wake, who was a most heroic and highly decorated French Resistance and special operations fighter during WWII. The modern day messaging application provides strong end-to-end encryption, decentralized peer-to-peer connections, and the ability to exchange messages via wifi or bluetooth. It incorporates smartly written code with security as a top priority in all aspects.

As a person who makes regular use of messaging applications, I find the current crop of user friendly and security oriented choices to be a very good trend. Session, White Mouse, and Element are especially good.

## Alternate Sources of Internet Besides the Local ISP

When internet service is unavailable due to government mandated shutdowns, natural disasters, or warfare, advocates have attempted to provide connectivity by alternate methods. Flying communications nodes aboard aircraft, balloons, and satellites have been successfully used in recent years.

Using radio to reach people in a denied area isn't especially new, having been a method of information warfare since the period leading up to WWII. Remember, information warfare has two aspects: domestic censorship, radio jamming (if effective), and pro-government messaging versus messaging directed to *external* audiences to *disinform and discourage* an adversary.

By latter years of the Cold War, the U.S. government's *Broadcasting Board of Governors* had been broadcasting programming created for an audience in Cuba, which the Cuban government regularly jammed. An aerostat, nicknamed *Fat Albert*, was sent up in 1990 to broadcast the VHF and UHF television signals of *TV Martí*.

Signals did indeed reach the people of Cuba at a usable signal strength, except the broadcasts were often rendered unwatchable due to jamming.

Aerostat, operated by the USAF

When the aerostat was destroyed by a hurricane in 2005, the U.S. government substituted a C-130 turboprop, replaced later by a Gulfstream I. Because of the jamming, TV Martí was dubbed, "la TV que no se ve," which translates to "the TV that no one sees." Budget cuts eliminated the airborne broadcasts in 2013.

That experience of airborne broadcasting teaches three lessons:

- aerostats work unless there is jamming
- aerostats are vulnerable to weather
- aircraft are too expensive for long term contact

Project Loon began during 2011, as a Google X research and development idea, seeking to deliver broadband internet from high altitude balloons to underserved rural areas in the world. For a decade, the project worked out numerous technical challenges, eventually creating a reliable and effective broadband data communications system. Loon's profit margin was too narrow to make a viable business, so it was discontinued.

However, Loon did several things which proved the usefulness of its methods. After Hurricane Maria knocked out power and phone service in Puerto Rico, Loon sent balloons to the region to provide data service to people with 4G phones. Internet service was provided by Loon's equipment high over Peru after terrestrial signals went silent due damage from an 8.0 magnitude earthquake.

Telkom, a phone service provider in Kenya, has received government approval to deploy Loon's internet balloon technology, blanketing rural areas with 4G broadband.

The technology works. As a censorship circumvention tool, it could certainly connect to compatible devices deep within a country's borders. Jamming mobile phone service would likely be too disruptive to implement.

Even better than internet from balloons is internet from satellites, and it truly worries the world's biggest autocracies. When Russia invaded Ukraine in early 2022, Ukranian military units made use of *Starlink* satellites, which operate from low Earth orbit. Fighting had knocked out a significant amount of terrestrial phone and internet service. Starlink broadband was fast enough, and had low enough latency, to provide useful data communications across the country.

A review written for Ookla, by Josh Fomon, compared speeds of conventional broadband and Starlink. In most countries proximate to Ukraine, subscribers to the satellite service enjoyed upload speeds exceeding 15 mbps and download speeds in excess off 95 mbps. Latency, a measure of the time delay within a network, was best with terrestrial services – measuring on average about 12 ms. Starlink, with signals traveling paths of hundreds of kilometers, had latencies measuring near 45 ms.

To keep things in perspective, I measured my terrestrial broadband performance from home and various places around town. Upload and download speeds varied with the subscriber service levels, but latencies (pinging Google DNS servers) were all consistently in the 60 ms to 80 ms range. When using VPNs, over very long distances, the latencies increased to about 400 ms or more.

Autocracies have grave worries about satellite internet services. Primarily, they are concerned that such services are censorship resistant. What are authorities to do, with no data centers or company executives to approach with censorship demands? Starlink satellites communicate via microwave backhauls with their ground stations and with each other via lasers – not needing facilities in hostile countries. There has even been talk of utilizing spare bandwidth of customer's rooftop terminals for operating a mesh network to augment the existing backhauls.

Already, we have an answer. The PRC has asked Starlink to not sell satellite terminals to the Chinese people. Obviously, they can ban Starlink. What is really being asked is to not sell Starlink in Taiwan, due to concerns that connectivity will be used there as it has been in Ukraine.

Bear in mind how many people live in autocracies and have heavily censored internet. Satellite internet companies may resist censorship demands of the most extremist dictators, but I believe that they will yield in order to acquire more subscribers. Censorship is just a matter of software, customer lists, and databases. Of course, circumvention is just a matter of software, encryption, and routing. Game on.

Suppose *things get really bad* and internet service is fully cut off or censored to the point of being unusable? In at least a handful of countries, the situation is *already* that bad. Consider the worst autocracies on our planet, those with the bottom Freedom Index scores.

When no other options remain, the bottom line is communicating via *sneakernet*, which means to carry files by hand on physical devices. Before electronic communications, we carried notes on paper or images in film canisters. In the current era, we may carry a whole library's measure of books on a tiny flash drive.

What's more, we may use an application like *Veracrypt* to make an encrypted volume with a hidden mini volume within. Put some junk files in the encrypted volume and the prohibited, censored data in the hidden mini volume. Inspectors would be none the wiser if a person crossed a border and showed what was in the non-hidden volume on a flash drive.

I routinely listen to lectures and convention speeches about censorship and how to defeat it. When the sneakernet is discussed, it is the secure messaging apps like Briar, Session, and Serval Chat which are mentioned. They will hold messages until detecting the presence of another node in the mesh, then send it to the newly discovered device. All it tales is two people with mesh networking phones in their pockets to pass one another on a street, and the data moves!

## Dealing with Criminals and Bad Actors

There are persons, other than honest, justice loving people like you and me, who drive demand for strong anonymity and privacy, with whom most of us are much less sympathetic.

It is a persistent problem that people engage in illicit behavior where they have cover. They trade or share stolen personal data, multimedia depicting gory accidents or violence, abuse of animals, elderly people, or children. Others buy and sell mind-altering substances in hidden markets. A rather robust group of fascists use the darknet to share instructions for making improvised weapons and trading stolen military equipment.

No darknet criminals will cease to exist if the privacy, anonymity, and anti-censorship tools are destroyed.

Law enforcement agencies throughout the world are capable of doing the necessary investigative work to put criminals away without a ban on VPNs or Tor. Mandating weak encryption or backdoors in the code only makes things easier for the bad guys.

Let the security and anonymity tools be effective, plentiful, and easy to use. I advocate these tools for normal everyday people to participate in free expression, make informed decisions about their lives, and to act against autocracy. We everyday people are on the right side of history and we will win. Maybe not tomorrow, but we will win.

# Chapter 6: Strategies and Metrics

Enabling people within closed and censored societies to have contact with the outside world – on their own terms – is the ultimate goal of circumventionism. Making censorship systems into irrelevant, heat generating, electricity wasting machines, is a short term goal.

An organized and rational way to attack censorship is to study its application. It is essential to learn how the system functions, where it is weak, and how to exploit the weaknesses. In other words, circumventionists must think like martial artist hackers. Imagine Bruce Lee or Muhammad Ali with a computer. Would such fighters mindlessly subscribe to a VPN and play server whack-a-mole for years? No they would apply a *Jeet Kune Do* or *Rope-a-dope* strategy, letting the attacker extend himself and make a decisive blunder. Winning the fight is a result of smartly applied Strategies!

What do we know about censorship strategies followed by censoring countries? One thing known for sure is that blacklisted items vary from regime to regime, also within regimes over time. Methods used against the blacklists are pretty consistent. It appears that the technology is developed by a small number of corporations or universities, then deployed in the leading autocracies. From there, censorship tools and methods are adopted by smaller allies.

Measures start with DNS poisoning, then IP address blockages, up to detection and blocking of proxies and VPNs. Some countries also require web browsers to have government issued root certificates, for surveillance of TLS protected web pages.

Modern information technology is a threat to autocrats. Yes, they may use it against free countries, as Russia and the PRC do against the West. But it is a double edged blade, as controlling the information environment at home has become much more difficult in the age of broadband and smartphones. What they really want is state of the art broadband for businesses and ratty dial-up performance for the personal use of citizens.

It is unrealistic to hope for citizens who are not very literate or good at critical thinking. Dictators are comfortable if the people simply work hard in their jobs, then use their internet to pay bills and share pictures of their pets. There is actually a *Cute Cat Theory*, which asserts that people are mostly not activists and prefer to use the internet for mundane tasks as described above. Another theory, called *bread and circuses,* says that people will be docile and satisfied if they have food, shelter, and simple entertainment.

I would argue a slightly different point: activists aren't born, but are made in adversity. It is police shakedowns and violence which energize such movements as the Arab Spring and Black Lives Matter protests. People can take moderate abuse for years, but there is always a time when the line is crossed and people are willing to fight back. An internet functional enough for sharing cute cat images is functional enough for activists to campaign for social and political change. People who believe things should be better than they are will use the internet to find out why. They'll reach out and find others of like mind. A censor who blocks their access or deletes their media postings has created yet another circumventionist.


**The Strategy of Plentiful Relays**

A most basic strategy for circumventing censorship is setting up plentiful encrypted routes through unblocked servers. It is the freshman course for internet unblocking with VPNs and proxies, with strength derived from diversity. This strategy depends on large numbers of non-blacklisted IP addresses being available for anti-censorship tools. For every VPN or proxy which is blocked, another one may be set up, and the sooner the better. When small numbers of users are involved, any specific VPN may run for several days before being blocked. My colleagues in the airline industry took advantage of that in Asia, the Middle East, and Africa; finding servers which worked, then switching to others when they stopped. The toughest censorship was in the PRC, where VPNs would work for any duration from a few hours to a day before being throttled, choked, and then fully blocked. It was a night versus day difference between being in Shanghai versus Taipei and connecting to SoundCloud or WordPress. From the former, connections were slow, as though on dialup, while broadband from the latter was lightning fast.

The necessity of having a large number of servers available, both in terms of IP addresses and physical locations, cannot be overemphasized. Free and open addresses must greatly outnumber the ones blacklisted, and a great many VPNs and proxies must be deployed. It is the cyber equivalent of an army depending on human wave attacks. It is expected that censors integrated within ISPs will detect the fingerprints of popular VPN protocols and block them. When a server falls, it is quickly replaced by the user with another. Truly, I would routinely prepare lists of VPN data at weekly intervals. VPN Gate had a lot of L2TP/IPsec servers, and I scraped their addresses from the main web site each week. I would also collect OpenVPN config files the same way other people collected cute cat pictures.

With a vast supply of VPN server information, I poked a thousand holes in the censorship where I lived and other places I visited. It is still true today that as long as the global internet is available on at least one gateway at the national border, *everything* can be found from *anywhere*.

Not only do VPNs and proxies benefit from existing in large numbers, but mesh networks also need to exist en masse. With more nodes, they are more broadband in nature. Experts who studied *Serval Mesh* and *Firechat* estimated a need of about eight percent of a population to operate network nodes in order for eighty five percent of the population to have connectivity. With lots of nodes, mesh networks are fast, offer solid coverage, and are self-healing.

## The Strategy of Collateral Freedom

The next major circumvention strategy has been mentioned before, called *Collateral Freedom*. A more familiar concept is collateral damage, which is a term used to describe harm to proximate bystanders or innocent people from a missile strike or bombing against a military target. Instead of harming something nearby, collateral freedom protects something nearby from harm. With regard to circumventionism, it means setting up servers with anti-censorship tools on the same IP addresses as things the countries depend on economically. For example, VPNs or Pluggable Transports are unlikely to be blocked if operating on IPs held by Microsoft Azure, Amazon AWS, Fastly, Cloudflare, and Akamai.

Collateral freedom considers the financial hardship suffered by a censoring country when sites are blocked. When there is no hardship, censors can be quite indiscriminate in blacklisting IP addresses. When large banks or financial services are impaired, authorities take notice and tend to be much more careful.

Collateral freedom is not a strategy limited to circumvention tools. Reporters Without Borders (RSF) has a continuing project which protects news sites by setting up website mirrors on servers operated by large internet companies. Mirrors are copies of a website which function if the original is blocked or offline. To block one of them would also take down essential domains which no developed country would want to forfeit.

**GreatFire** is an organization of people strongly supportive of collateral freedom. It has set up several sites for unblocked access from censored countries, created a web browser which unblocks everything via collateral freedom, and even created an appmaker which others may use to create Android programs which are not hampered by censorship.

Collateral freedom has been designed into a lot of applications which are in use today. They tend to function either as robust communication tools or as a circumvention layer for other communication tools on a device.

**Psiphon** is circumvention system which uses "SSH wrapped in obfuscated SSH" to pass data between clients and a centrally managed group of thousands of servers. Connections start with the client reaching out to several servers at once, to find which are the fastest. Psiphon updates its server list and tries to establish a route to the client's desired egress country.

To prevent an attacker from knowing where to find all of the servers, only a small subset is revealed clients. Psiphon logs data about the clients connection time and locations, for purposes of advertising.

Another popular circumvention system is **Lantern**, which uses https proxies to connect clients to the global internet. Servers are set up in two groups: ones with domain fronting and the others running as peer-hosted modules on devices located in free countries.

Lantern uses a centralized infrastructure for authenticating users and assigning proxies, which could be a weakness if an attacker could find and block it. There is also a fallback capability, with which clients may find alternate routes through unblocked proxies to reach that infrastructure.

Lantern has a better privacy policy than Psiphon, logging no data which would disclose the identity or location of users. No time stamps, no browser history, and no DNS queries.

In my own experience, I have used Psiphon and Lantern for years and been pleased with the results. They are consistently able to reach the global internet, even in a multilayered censorship environment as found in China. Their free services are not especially broadbanded, but okay for basic browsing. Upgrading to paid services provides faster speeds.

For better security and much faster speeds, consider getting an inexpensive virtual private server, or possibly a real, bare metal server, located in a place with internet freedom.

## The Strategy of Refraction Networking

Even more cunning than domain fronting is a method of circumvention known as *Refraction Networking*. Sometimes referred to as "decoy routing," it was independently invented by teams of researchers at the University of Michigan, the University of Illinois and Raytheon BBN Technologies.

It was an answer to the question of, "how else could we embed a communication scheme so deeply within the internet that it would be infeasible to block?" The deeper embed turned out to be within the network's backbone, along routes to well known, unblocked websites (serving as decoys). The strategy involves the client sending innocuously appearing requests, but with special tags recognizable by a specially configured backbone server. When the server detects the tag, it changes into proxy mode and reroutes the request to a blocked website.

As seen from the censorship system, the data exchange would appear to be a normal one. What's more, if the censors were to try active probing, nothing unusual would be found.

Everyone loves a clever theory; making it work in the real world requires substantial effort. Not only must the outgoing requests look normal to the censors, but the return data must also be reasonable. That means packet sequence numbers, sizes, and even the latency must be consistent with visits to the decoy site.

Data coming in from the blocked site must be concealed in a smart manner. It could be hidden in irregular things such as images, video, or other data.

Four implementations of refraction networking are especially interesting:

- Telex – a collateral freedom project which evolved into refraction networking, also giving birth to the term "end to middle (E2M) proxying."

- TapDance - hides requests for blocked content within specially tagged requests for unblocked content. The requests are recognized by cooperating servers, which refracts the connection to reach blocked content.

- Slitheen - sneaks data past the censors by disguising data from blocked sites within images from unblocked sites.

- Conjure – refraction networking which uses unused address space instead of decoy sites. More deployable than older schemes.

It is great to see new ways to accomplish the business of censorship circumvention. Refraction networking has potential to accelerate the mission of making global connectivity trivially easy for anyone, anywhere, at any time.

## Taking Metrics on Censorship

Destroying the ability of authoritarian regimes to censor the internet and brainwash their populations is a dynamic enterprise. Things change on a weekly basis sometimes. Shutdowns start, shutdowns end. The GFW blocks more sites, then an updated pluggable transport unlocks those same sites. Things change. Here are some great sources of information on how things are going in the world of censorship and its circumvention.

**Netblocks** operates out of the United Kingdom and keeps a global watch on the internet. It keeps a regular stream of news running on its Twitter feed, including regional outages, restored service, safe networking tips, and related items. From time to time, Netblocks publishes in depth analysis of events related to news seen in its news stream.

**Open Observatory of Network Interference (OONI)** is a non-profit free software project that aims to empower decentralized efforts in documenting internet censorship around the world. They provide software for measuring the blocking and throttling of websites, messenger applications, and circumvention tools.

OONI publishes real-time analysis of internet measurements. If there is a question about a possible Tor outage, check with OONI. The observatory also publishes reports about internet censorship events which happen in various places around the world.

**GreatFire** is an anonymous organization based in China, focused on several aspects of online censorship and circumvention. They very actively monitor developments related to GFW censorship and promote circumventionist projects.

GreatFire links to several very useful tools for evading censorship, reading deleted posts from Chinese social media, and evaluating which sites are working or blocked. They even have a list of freshly updated VPN test results.

**CensorBib** is not the sort of bib one wears when having a meal of steamed crabs. Rather, it is a bibliography. It is a deep resource of scholarly research papers covering the topics of Internet censorship measurement and circumvention. It has works published as early as 1996, on up through the current day of this writing.

Other online sources which cover internet policies, censorship, and connectivity are listed in Appendix 4: Web Resources. Ultimately, you know your tools are good if they still work tomorrow.

## Recurring Issues and Persistence of Censorship

From time to time, suspicious events occur which arouse suspicions that either Russia or the PRC are playing dirty tricks to deanonymize Tor users or grab traffic destined for geopolitical adversaries.

One suspicious event happened on November 12, 2018. Traffic which was expected to move through Google's Cloud Platform went instead through Nigeria, China, and Russia.

MainOne (an Equinix Company) ✔ @Mainoneservice        13 Nov 2018

We have investigated the advertisement of @Google prefixes through one of our upstream partners. This was an error during a planned network upgrade due to a misconfiguration on our BGP filters. The error was corrected within 74mins & processes put in place to avoid reoccurrence

Nov 13, 2018 · 8:53 AM UTC

💬 1    ↻ 1    ⦂⦂    ♥

MainOne (an Equinix Company) ✔ @Mainoneservice        15 Nov 2018

Replying to @Mainoneservice @Google

Thank you for your support and understanding. We assure you of our continued commitment to the high degree of trust that makes the internet work efficiently. Please read our full update here bit.ly/2QJAezj

💬    ↻    ⦂⦂    ♥ 1

A deliberate hack of the Border Gateway Protocol (BGP) was suspected soon after the event began, as it is an effective way to either intercept or disrupt traffic.

I recall seeing speculation about the event on Twitter, with concerns that the PRC was attempting to get a high value Tor user or bust some activists. What appears to have happened was that Main One, a Nigerian ISP, mistakenly claimed a block if IP addresses which were actually slated for Google. The internet went haywire until the misconfiguration was fixed 74 minutes later.

On multiple and repeated occasions, there have been brief instances of China Telecom's Point of Presence (PoP) equipment being involved in BGP leaks. On June 6, 2019, another newsworthy event happened in Europe, in which 70,000 routes leaked from Switzerland's Safe Host to China Telecom's PoP in Frankfurt, Germany.

There is a distinct pattern of spokesperson responses to these events, along the lines of, "Whoops, sorry. Inadvertent error." As an internet user and advocate of circumventionism, all I can offer for advice is, "hope for good luck and don't ever believe in accidents or coincidences."

A much more cold and deliberate pattern of redirecting the internet is happening in Ukraine. Residents in the war torn country, like other people in the world, rely on network connectivity to keep in touch with loved ones and to share information about what is happening from day to day. When the invading Russian forces move into an area, a high priority task is to sever connections from Ukraine and patch the area in to the Russian network.

Ukranians managing regional ISP facilities often did what they could to thwart a successful redirection of network service, including destruction of equipment or wiping of firmware. Ukrtelecom CEO Yuriy Kurmaz said to Bloomberg News in July of 2022, "We will never collaborate."

Control of the internet therefore tends to follow whoever has control of the turf. Currently, the line of control is being pushed eastward toward borders existing before the war, possibly reaching the border as it was before little green men entered Crimea in 2014.

I offer a short comment here, "Putin Khuilo! Slava Ukraini!" Also, for what it's worth, satellite internet is available – but is a bit pricey at the present time.

If you find yourself in a land affected by war, be prepared for phone and network outages, and possibly a redirect under control of the combatants who have the territory. If the network works, consider using a strong privacy and anonymity network like Tor or I2p; assume your data packets are being subjected to deep packet inspection by people who are capable of causing great harm for no reason or any reason.

Regional shutdowns, as described earlier, continue to be a persistent problem in numerous countries, especially but not limited to India. Outages may be tracked with online news sources such as Netblocks and OONI. To stay connected, consider participating or leading in the set up of wireless mesh networks in your neighborhood or town. Also, consider using a mesh capable messaging application.

If you are lucky enough to be in an area with international appeal, or near the national border, balloon or aircraft-based internet may be available. This time is still early in the history of internet delivery from high altitudes. Of course, satellite internet is already available and may be an option to consider.

Last, but not least, as a solution to internet shutdowns, consider the sneakernet. Files may be transferred with certain mesh networking or peer-to-peer messenger applications mentioned earlier. Never be afraid to walk your data to a safe place if you need to.

Many of the persistent problems I have mentioned in this chapter are caused by very well funded bad actors. Billionaire oligarchs in the East and West are attacking democracies, hoping to destroy free expression and other human rights. Democracies are not free of blame in today's situation, as Western companies have sold plenty of spyware, malware, weapons, and censorship equipment to the bad actors deploying such tools.

**Actually, as long as there are humans, there are human rights.**

# Chapter 7: Commitment

Of all living things, human beings are the most stubborn. Perhaps it is because we have the ability to think about so much that is *not* rooted in the present moment. The pigeons, cats, and blades of grass which live around my residence don't get hung up on things they cannot see. They are lucky to take each day as it comes; they do not worry. All of us people are burdened with not only the now, but what was and what may be. People who seek power (all of the power) and wealth (all of the wealth) are manipulating us with worry. We are easily manipulated because we stubbornly cling to misinformation and disinformation we have been told over generational time spans.

My first fleeting thoughts of writing this book happened years ago, as I was seeing censorship and propaganda up close. Censorship was not something written about in a newspaper, but instead something personally experienced. It was the obstacle standing in my way. I am stubborn too, and censorship was something I was never going to accept. The way I see it, we are all the same stardust, carbon older than this planet; carbon older than the sun. Nobody is telling me what to think, say, not say, believe, or not believe. Even if this hour is my last hour, it is going to be an hour without subjugation. This book expresses an understanding that the same right of free thought and expression belongs to all people.

I knew a person who said to me, from time to time, "you can take yourself out of Baltimore, but nothing's gonna take the Baltimore out of you." It was true. As maddening as the statement was, it is true. It was a recognition of my own stubborn refusal to sit down and be cooperative with the sorts of authoritarians we know in our lives. Perhaps it is the heroes I have admired since my discovery of heroes.

Being from Baltimore was a blessing. It was proximate to places of significance in my development of concepts about heroism. My mother and grandparents were interested in American Civil war history. We went on road trips to visit Gettysburg, where the largest battle yet fought in the western hemisphere was fought. When the great cemetery was dedicated there, President Lincoln stood among the people and spoke of being at war to preserve the country founded on the awareness that "all men are created equal."

Being from Baltimore, I was fortunate to be so close to Washington DC and spend time there and see historically important places. I stood in the area where President Kennedy spoke during his inauguration, recognizing that our rights as human beings come not from the generosity of any state, but from God. Beyond that, a generation was afoot which was "unwilling to witness or permit the slow undoing of those human rights" to which the USA was said to be committed.

I would argue that to be "committed" has various shadings. Kennedy did not live to see the country truly become committed to human rights within its borders, when passage of the Civil Rights Act of 1964 and Voting Rights Act of 1965 were signed into law. Becoming committed was at the cost of a great many lives. Let us explore the concept of commitment.

In a 2014 talk on the subject of ethical leadership, Colonel Leo Thorsness - former fighter pilot and prisoner of war - spoke of his time in captivity. During the period when he and his fellow prisoners were kept in solitary confinement, they were prohibited from communicating. Anyone trying to communicate was punished with severe beatings. Despite the personal risk, they devised a tap code and regularly communicated through the walls. On Sundays, the most senior prisoner would send a message, forwarded by others throughout the network of cells: one tap, followed by three, sent twice (• •••   • •••). It meant "CC" for church call. During church call, the solitary prisoners would pray or contemplate spiritually.

# Hanoi Hilton Tap Code

Prisoners were prohibited from communicating. There was no way to use international Morse code through walls, but tapping worked. They developed a code based on a 5 x 5 grid of rows and columns, with "K" removed:

$$
\begin{array}{ccccc}
A & B & C & D & E \\
F & G & H & I & J \\
L & M & N & O & P \\
Q & R & S & T & U \\
V & W & X & Y & Z \\
\end{array}
$$

A common affirmation, "God bless you," was abbreviated as "GBU" and tapped through the walls by row and column for each letter (2-2, 1-2, 4-5):

•• ••   • ••   ••••   •••••

Thorsness told a story about "commitment" which happened later during captivity, when the prisoners were out of solitary and kept together in groups. They were prohibited from talking, especially from expressions of their religious faith. If anyone began to lead the group in a speaking of the *Lord's Prayer*, guards would enter the cell, remove the person, and administer a beating in an area of punishment cells known as *heartbreak*. The senior prisoner at the time was Edwin A. Shuman III. Thorsness related that Shuman challenged each prisoner with the question, "Are you committed.?" Of course, the expected answer was "yes."

Having established commitment of each person, Shuman led the men in challenging the rule against prayer. He stood up, calling out, "Gentlemen, the Lord's Prayer!" They would begin reciting it, which was soon followed by Shuman being taking out to heartbreak for a beating. In order of seniority, one by one, the men loudly stood and began the prayer, saw the leader taken out to heartbreak by the guards, and repeated the cycle. After five of the men had been worked over by the guards, the guards stopped the beatings and permitted Sunday prayer. A win for the prisoners. Commitment was a matter of doing the right thing, even when one was at personal risk.

Commitment is really a two part issue. What are you willing to take responsibility for, which may cost you blood or money? It is not as clear as deciding what you would die for; sometimes it is a matter of what you would (or would not) do to *other people*. It can be a question of what will you put your soul on the line for. All things end in reckoning, and when it is all measured up, it is so much better to keep the faith, to do right - even to the last measure.

Another favorite place of mine in Washington is at the opposite end of the National Mall, past the museums, which are the grounds around the Capitol building. It was within the Capitol where President Franklin D. Roosevelt made his "Four Freedoms" speech. At the time, the USA was nearing involvement in the second global war being fought against authoritarians who were resolutely committed AGAINST the truth that all of us were created equal. Seven years earlier, Roosevelt was almost overthrown in a scheme we now call the "Business Plot," in which an extremely wealthy group of men with far-right ideology conspired to overthrow the elected government and establish an autocracy. America could very well have been ruled by nightmarish people sympathetic to Hitler and Hirohito.

FDR took the heroic position in opposition to autocracy. He observed that mankind was becoming more capable of solving long existing problems, and at the same time gaining capability of inflicting harm on a large scale. In the USA and Europe, fascism had found allies in the pseudo scientific eugenics movement, which labeled other humans as unworthy of living. They had united under the banner of improving humanity by eliminating people not of the master race.

FDR, in 1941, saw the emergence of information warfare which was being waged in newspapers, radio broadcasts, and from extremist church pulpits:

"Every realist knows that the democratic way of life is at this moment being directly assailed in every part of the world-- assailed either by arms, or by secret spreading of poisonous propaganda by those who seek to destroy unity and promote discord in nations that are still at peace."

FDR was too polite to stand up before congress and scream, "Bullcrap!" He simply drew in some breath and spoke, enumerating these points:

> "In the future days, which we seek to make secure, we look forward to a world founded upon four essential human freedoms.
>
> The first is freedom of speech and expression-- everywhere in the world.
>
> The second is freedom of every person to worship God in his own way--everywhere in the world.
>
> The third is freedom from want--which, translated into

104

world terms, means economic understandings which will secure to every nation a healthy peacetime life for its inhabitants-everywhere in the world.

The fourth is freedom from fear--which, translated into world terms, means a world-wide reduction of armaments to such a point and in such a thorough fashion that no nation will be in a position to commit an act of physical aggression against any neighbor--anywhere in the world.

That is no vision of a distant millennium. It is a definite basis for a kind of world attainable in our own time and generation. That kind of world is the very antithesis of the so-called new order of tyranny which the dictators seek to create with the crash of a bomb."

As I write these words, those four freedoms are not known to about 72% of the world, and a more fair accounting could put the percentage closer to 80%. It was censorship I encountered on trips to the Middle East and through parts of Asia which motivated me to become proficient in using circumvention technology. Airline executives would admonish us line pilots, calling on us to "respect the local laws" and explicitly warning us not use VPNs to stream the BBC or other blocked content. My position has always been, "freedom expression belongs to me, anywhere." Actually, freedom of expression belongs to every person.

After all of that, about a third of the people in my home country seek to elect a fascist government, appoint fascist judges, and attack basic human rights. Those same people attacked the Capitol where FDR spoke of the four freedoms. They are all over the country, making loud efforts to close libraries, block websites they don't like, impose Christian nationalist ideology on schools, and destroy what is left of the health care system. People like me have no intention of allowing that to go uncontested.

When I assembled the set of circumvention tools for my usage overseas, called *MOFO Linux*, I could not have dreamed that it could be of use against censorship in the USA. But we are in some interesting times, and the red states are interesting places. If people want to play censorship games, people like me have the tools to nullify it. If we are in a "post truth" world, then it may just as easily be a "post censorship" world.

Autocrats are never short of reasons to spread disinformation and attack truth. They do it everywhere. Because even the free countries are targeted for information warfare where dictators cannot censor, there is no place on Earth without at least a tinge of disinformation in the air. Because of the significant presence of disinformation used to attack free countries, if you break out of a splinternet to find some Western media, be careful and evaluate what you find. Don't go on American WebSDR sites to tune in extremist far-right mediumwave stations. Don't break out of internet jail just to find a video site which feeds you streams of fascist content just as bad as in your home splinternet.

The biggest problem with information warfare is that a successful campaign makes truth irrelevant. As a target, you may lose awareness of what is true. If you do remember what is true, you may lose motivation to act on it. Why bother? It is easier to get along and go along... If you ever feel that way, remember Leo Thorsness, Ned Shuman, and the other prisoners who took beatings rather than give up their resistance.

**If this hour is your last hour, make it one of self-respect and courageous resistance.**

In his April 16, 1963 Letter From Birmingham Jail, Reverend Dr. Martin Luther King Jr. was critical of people with moderate or centrist leanings, who wanted a slower pace of progress. He asserted that "injustice anywhere is a threat to justice everywhere."

Moderates were willing to accept a measure of injustice, which was to be suffered by people other than themselves. Where is the commitment? Without personal risk, there is no commitment. As to information warfare, I argue here that disinformation anywhere is a threat to truth everywhere. Censorship anywhere is a threat to free expression everywhere. We cannot simply compromise by drawing a line and agree to not cross it, as the fight over where to draw the line does not ever end. Until the line is gone.

No person is obligated to accept being lied to. When nation-states insist on feeding untruths to the people, the people have options to to reject it and continue to find what is real. Every censorship system has weaknesses which may be exploited. For example, blacklists may be circumvented with technologies like Tor, VPNs, or Shadowsocks. Shutdowns can be circumvented with peer-to-peer mesh networking, either with wifi or bluetooth. Some people will simply out wait the shutdown. Others will turn to satellite services or walk data around the sneakernet.

It is surprising how many people do not understand how censorship regimes are destined to fail. Perhaps the good news is that there is no longer a dictatorship where truth is completely hidden. I am heartened to hear that even in North Korea, there is a working sneakernet. Also, there is circumvention of radio censorship, where hackers are finding ways to modify radios so that they may tune to frequencies other than official DPRK media.

The world appears to be sorting itself into a bipolar arrangement of power-oriented versus truth-oriented people. Myths which support autocracies are appealing to some people, who believe power matters than truth. The same, right leaning people also believe loyalty matters more than competence.

People who live by truth must be students of disinformation and circumvention. It is necessary to identify sources, know the families of talking points, and how to best nullify their effects. Become expert users of circumvention tools. When media is banned, make the bans fail. When autocrats tell lies, expose them.

Autocratic countries are no longer able to to 100% censor and brainwash. Conversely, democracies are not able to 100% eliminate disinformation. In both cases, people are sorting between power and truth orientations. Information warfare may be with us for a long time into the future, in a manner similar to the persistence of eugenic pseudo science and fundamentalist religions.

Let us think for a moment or two about colors. at the long wavelength end of the visible spectrum, there is red. At the short wavelength end, there is blue, then violet. People who are discussing politics, social issues, and governance in the United States often illustrate their points with maps. On the maps, there are red states, very Republican or right-leaning. Then there are blue states, very Democratic and left-leaning. Then there are so-called swing states, which are sometimes characterized as purple.

Purple is an illusion. Purple is what we perceive when red pigment is so close to blue that our eyes cannot separate them, and our rods send a mixed signal to our brains. On those red and blue maps, a look with a larger scale reveals areas of red proximate to areas of blue. Often, the cities are areas of high populations, with Democratic Party orientation. Around the cities there are a lot of red areas, with lesser population densities, oriented with the Republicans. They are different and don't really mix much.

Don't plan on the emergence of a mythic utopia filled with people who look and think the same. It is more true to understand that we humans have a lot of small differences as well as plenty in common. To overcome the ancient dogmas and nineteenth century falsehoods which drove the majority of twentieth century violence, we need to orient toward accepting twenty-first century truth and reasoning. Autocrats intend to use the old prejudices and hates to divide people and then take wealth and power for their own benefit. Analysis of information warfare around the world shows exactly that.

If we stubborn human beings can find a way to live by truth, we can have justice. With justice, we can have peace. With peace, we can have progress. Those ends are far more likely when average people have effective anti-censorship measures readily available. Make no compromises. Take no prisoners. Be committed.

# Appendix 1: The Conscience of a Hacker

*Written by The Mentor (Loyd Blankenship), January 8, 1986*

Another one got caught today, it's all over the papers. "Teenager Arrested in Computer Crime Scandal", "Hacker Arrested after Bank Tampering"...

Damn kids. They're all alike.

But did you, in your three-piece psychology and 1950's technobrain, ever take a look behind the eyes of the hacker? Did you ever wonder what made him tick, what forces shaped him, what may have molded him?

I am a hacker, enter my world...

Mine is a world that begins with school... I'm smarter than most of the other kids, this crap they teach us bores me...

Damn underachiever. They're all alike.

I'm in junior high or high school. I've listened to teachers explain for the fifteenth time how to reduce a fraction. I understand it. "No, Ms. Smith, I didn't show my work. I did it in my head..."

Damn kid. Probably copied it. They're all alike.


I made a discovery today. I found a computer. Wait a second, this is cool. It does what I want it to. If it makes a mistake, it's because I screwed it up. Not because it doesn't like me...

Or feels threatened by me...

Or thinks I'm a smart ass...

Or doesn't like teaching and shouldn't be here...

Damn kid. All he does is play games. They're all alike.


And then it happened... a door opened to a world... rushing through the phone line like heroin through an addict's veins, an electronic pulse is sent out, a refuge from the day-to-day incompetencies is sought... a board is found.

"This is it... this is where I belong..."

I know everyone here... even if I've never met them, never talked to them, may never hear from them again... I know you all...

Damn kid. Tying up the phone line again. They're all alike...


You bet your ass we're all alike... we've been spoon-fed baby food at school when we hungered for steak... the bits of meat that you did let slip through were pre-chewed and tasteless. We've been dominated by sadists, or ignored by the apathetic. The few that had something to teach found us willing pupils, but those few are like drops of water in the desert.

## Censorship's Grave

This is our world now... the world of the electron and the switch, the beauty of the baud.  We make use of a service already existing without paying for what could be dirt-cheap if it wasn't run by profiteering gluttons, and you call us criminals.  We explore... and you call us criminals.  We seek after knowledge... and you call us criminals.  We exist without skin color, without nationality, without religious bias... and you call us criminals. You build atomic bombs, you wage wars, you murder, cheat, and lie to us and try to make us believe it's for our own good, yet we're the criminals.

Yes, I am a criminal.  My crime is that of curiosity.  My crime is that of judging people by what they say and think, not what they look like. My crime is that of outsmarting you, something that you will never forgive me for.

I am a hacker, and this is my manifesto.  You may stop this individual, but you can't stop us all... after all, we're all alike.

# Appendix 2: A Declaration for the Future of the Internet

*Declaration signed by more than 60 countries, circa 2022.*

We are united by a belief in the potential of digital technologies to promote connectivity, democracy, peace, the rule of law, sustainable development, and the enjoyment of human rights and fundamental freedoms. As we increasingly work, communicate, connect, engage, learn, and enjoy leisure time using digital technologies, our reliance on an open, free, global, interoperable, reliable, and secure Internet will continue to grow. Yet we are also aware of the risks inherent in that reliance and the challenges we face.

We call for a new Declaration for the Future of the Internet that includes all partners who actively support a future for the Internet that is an open, free, global, interoperable, reliable, and secure. We further affirm our commitment to protecting and respecting human rights online and across the digital ecosystem. Partners in this Declaration intend to work toward an environment that reinforces our democratic systems and promotes active participation of every citizen in democratic processes, secures and protects individuals' privacy, maintains secure and reliable connectivity, resists efforts to splinter the global Internet, and promotes a free and competitive global economy. Partners in this Declaration invite other partners who share this vision to join us in working together, with civil society and other stakeholders, to affirm guiding principles for our role in the future of the global Internet.

## Reclaiming the Promise of the Internet

The immense promise that accompanied the development of the Internet stemmed from its design: it is an open "network of networks", a single interconnected communications system for all of humanity. The stable and secure operation of the Internet's unique identifier systems have, from the beginning, been governed by a multistakeholder approach to avoid Internet fragmentation, which continues to be an essential part of our vision. For business, entrepreneurs, and the innovation ecosystem as a whole, interconnection promises better access to customers and fairer competition; for artists and creators, new audiences; for everyone, unfettered access to knowledge. With the creation of the Internet came a swell in innovation, vibrant communication, increased cross-border data flows, and market growth—as well as the invention of new digital products and services that now permeate every aspect of our daily lives.

Over the last two decades, however, we have witnessed serious challenges to this vision emerge. Access to the open Internet is limited by some authoritarian governments and online platforms and digital tools are increasingly used to repress freedom of expression and deny other human rights and fundamental freedoms. State-sponsored or condoned malicious behavior is on the rise, including the spread of disinformation and cybercrimes such as ransomware, affecting the security and the resilience of critical infrastructure while holding at risk vital public and private assets. At the same time, countries have erected firewalls and taken other technical measures, such as Internet shutdowns, to restrict access to journalism, information, and services, in ways that are contrary to international human rights commitments and obligations. Concerted or independent actions of some governments and private actors have sought to abuse the openness of Internet governance and related processes to advance a closed vision. Moreover, the once decentralized Internet economy has become highly concentrated and many people have legitimate concerns about their privacy and the quantity and security of personal data collected and stored online. Online platforms have enabled an increase in the spread of illegal or harmful content that can threaten the safety of individuals and contribute to radicalization and violence. Disinformation and foreign malign activity is used to sow division and conflict between individuals or groups in society, undermining respect for and protection of human rights and democratic institutions.

## Our Vision

We believe we should meet these challenges by working towards a shared vision for the future of the Internet that recommits governments and relevant authorities to defending human rights and fostering equitable economic prosperity. We intend to ensure that the use of digital technologies reinforces, not weakens, democracy and respect for human rights; offers opportunities for innovation in the digital ecosystem, including businesses large and small; and, maintains connections between our societies. We intend to work together to protect and fortify the multistakeholder system of Internet governance and to maintain a high level of security, privacy protection, stability and resilience of the technical infrastructure of the Internet.

We affirm our commitment to promote and sustain an Internet that: is an open, free, global, interoperable, reliable, and secure and to ensure that the Internet reinforces democratic principles and human rights and fundamental freedoms; offers opportunities for collaborative research and commerce; is developed, governed, and deployed in an inclusive way so that unserved and underserved communities, particularly those coming online for the first time, can navigate it safely and with personal data privacy and protections in place; and is governed by multistakeholder processes. In short, an Internet that can deliver on the promise of connecting humankind and helping societies and democracies to thrive.

The Internet should operate as a single, decentralized network of networks – with global reach and governed through the multistakeholder approach, whereby governments and relevant authorities partner with academics, civil society, the private sector, technical community and others. Digital technologies reliant on the Internet, will yield the greatest dividends when they operate as an open, free, global, interoperable, reliable, and secure systems. Digital technologies should be produced, used, and governed in ways that enable trustworthy, free, and fair commerce; avoid unfair discrimination between, and ensure effective choice for, individual users; foster fair competition and encourage innovation; promote and protect human rights; and, foster societies where:

- Human rights and fundamental freedoms, and the well-being of all individuals are protected and promoted;

- All can connect to the Internet, no matter where they are located, including through increased access, affordability, and digital skills;

- Individuals and businesses can trust the safety and the confidentiality of the digital technologies they use and that their privacy is protected; Businesses of all sizes can innovate, compete, and thrive on their merits in a fair and competitive ecosystem;

- Infrastructure is designed to be secure, interoperable, reliable, and sustainable;

- Technology is used to promote pluralism and freedom of expression, sustainability, inclusive economic growth, and the fight against global climate change.

# Principles to promote this Vision

The partners in this Declaration intend to uphold a range of key principles, set out below, regarding the Internet and digital technologies; to promote these principles within existing multilateral and multistakeholder fora; to translate these principles into concrete policies and actions; and, work together to promote this vision globally, while respecting each other's regulatory autonomy within our own jurisdictions and in accordance with our respective domestic laws and international legal obligations. These principles are not legally binding but should rather be used as a reference for public policy makers, as well as citizens, businesses, and civil society organizations.

## Protection of Human Rights and Fundamental Freedoms

- Dedicate ourselves, in conducting and executing our respective domestic authorities, to respect human rights, including as reflected in the Universal Declaration of Human Rights, as well as the principles of the rule of law, legitimate purpose, non-arbitrariness, effective oversight, and transparency, both online and offline, and call upon others to do the same.

- Promote online safety and continue to strengthen our work to combat violence online, including sexual and gender-based violence as well as child sexual exploitation, to make the Internet a safe and secure place for everyone, particularly women, children, and young people.

- Promote safe and equitable use of the Internet for everyone, without discrimination based on sex, race, color, ethnic, national or social origin, genetic features, language, religion or belief, political or any other opinion, membership of an indigenous population, property, birth,

117

disability, age, gender identity or sexual orientation.

- Reaffirm our commitment that actions taken by governments, authorities, and digital services including online platforms to reduce illegal and harmful content and activities online be consistent with international human rights law, including the right to freedom of expression while encouraging diversity of opinion, and pluralism without fear of censorship, harassment, or intimidation.

- Protect and respect human rights and fundamental freedoms across the digital ecosystem, while providing access to meaningful remedies for human rights violations and abuses, consistent with international human rights law.

- Refrain from misusing or abusing the Internet or algorithmic tools or techniques for unlawful surveillance, oppression, and repression that do not align with international human rights principles, including developing social score cards or other mechanisms of domestic social control or pre-crime detention and arrest.

## A Global Internet

- Refrain from government-imposed internet shutdowns or degrading domestic Internet access, either entirely or partially. Refrain from blocking or degrading access to lawful content, services, and applications on the Internet, consistent with principles of Net Neutrality subject to applicable law, including international human rights law.

- Promote our work to realize the benefits of data free flows with trust based on our shared values as like-minded, democratic, open and outward looking partners.

- Promote cooperation in research and innovation and standard setting, encourage information sharing regarding security threats through relevant international fora, and reaffirm our commitment to the framework of responsible state behavior in cyberspace.

## Inclusive and Affordable Access to the Internet

- Promote affordable, inclusive, and reliable access to the Internet for individuals and businesses where they need it and support efforts to close digital divides around the world to ensure all people of the world are able to benefit from the digital transformation.

- Support digital literacy, skills acquisition, and development so that individuals can overcome the digital divide, participate in the Internet safely, and realize the economic and social potential of the digital economy.

- Foster greater exposure to diverse cultural and multilingual content, information, and news online. Exposure to diverse content online should contribute to pluralistic public discourse, foster greater social and digital inclusion within society, bolster resilience to disinformation and misinformation, and increase participation in democratic processes.

## Trust in the Digital Ecosystem

- Work together to combat cybercrime, including cyber-enabled crime, and deter malicious cyber activity.

- Ensure that government and relevant authorities' access to personal data is based in law and conducted in accordance with international human rights law.

- Protect individuals' privacy, their personal data, the confidentiality of electronic communications and information on end-users' electronic devices, consistent with the protection of public safety and applicable domestic and international law.

- Promote the protection of consumers, in particular vulnerable consumers, from online scams and other unfair practices online and from dangerous and unsafe products sold online.

- Promote and use trustworthy network infrastructure and services suppliers, relying on risk-based assessments that include technical and non-technical factors for network security.

- Refrain from using the Internet to undermine the electoral infrastructure, elections and political processes, including through covert information manipulation campaigns.

- Support a rules-based global digital economy which fosters trade and contestable and fair online markets so that firms and entrepreneurs can compete on their merits.

- Cooperate to maximize the enabling effects of technology for combatting climate change and protecting the environment whilst reducing as much as possible the environmental footprint of the Internet and digital technologies.

## Multistakeholder Internet Governance

- Protect and strengthen the multistakeholder system of Internet governance, including the development, deployment, and management of its main technical protocols and other related standards and protocols.

- Refrain from undermining the technical infrastructure essential to the general availability and integrity of the Internet.

We believe that the principles for the future of the Internet are universal in nature and as such we invite those who share this vision to affirm these principles and join us in the implementation of this vision. This Declaration takes into account, and expects to contribute to, existing processes in the UN system, G7, G20, the Organisation for Economic Cooperation and Development, the World Trade Organization, and other relevant multilateral and multistakeholder fora, the Internet Corporation for Assigned Names and Numbers, Internet Governance Forum, and Freedom Online Coalition. We also welcome partnership with the many civil society organizations essential to promoting an open, free, global, interoperable, reliable, and secure Internet, and defending fundamental freedoms and human rights online. Partners in this Declaration intend to consult and work closely with stakeholders in carrying forward this vision.

# Appendix 3: A Declaration of the Independence of Cyberspace

*Published by John Perry Barlow (1947-2018), February 8, 1996*

Governments of the Industrial World, you weary giants of flesh and steel, I come from Cyberspace, the new home of Mind. On behalf of the future, I ask you of the past to leave us alone. You are not welcome among us. You have no sovereignty where we gather.

We have no elected government, nor are we likely to have one, so I address you with no greater authority than that with which liberty itself always speaks. I declare the global social space we are building to be naturally independent of the tyrannies you seek to impose on us. You have no moral right to rule us nor do you possess any methods of enforcement we have true reason to fear.

Governments derive their just powers from the consent of the governed. You have neither solicited nor received ours. We did not invite you. You do not know us, nor do you know our world. Cyberspace does not lie within your borders. Do not think that you can build it, as though it were a public construction project. You cannot. It is an act of nature and it grows itself through our collective actions.

You have not engaged in our great and gathering conversation, nor did you create the wealth of our marketplaces. You do not know our culture, our ethics, or the unwritten codes that already provide our society more order than could be obtained by any of your impositions.

You claim there are problems among us that you need to solve. You use this claim as an excuse to invade our precincts. Many of these problems don't exist. Where there are real conflicts, where there are wrongs, we will identify them and address them by our means. We are forming our own Social Contract. This governance will arise according to the conditions of our world, not yours. Our world is different.

Cyberspace consists of transactions, relationships, and thought itself, arrayed like a standing wave in the web of our communications. Ours is a world that is both everywhere and nowhere, but it is not where bodies live.

We are creating a world that all may enter without privilege or prejudice accorded by race, economic power, military force, or station of birth.

We are creating a world where anyone, anywhere may express his or her beliefs, no matter how singular, without fear of being coerced into silence or conformity.

Your legal concepts of property, expression, identity, movement, and context do not apply to us. They are all based on matter, and there is no matter here.

Our identities have no bodies, so, unlike you, we cannot obtain order by physical coercion. We believe that from ethics, enlightened self-interest, and the commonweal, our governance will emerge. Our identities may be distributed across many of your jurisdictions. The only law that all our constituent cultures would generally recognize is the Golden Rule. We hope we will be able to build our particular solutions on that basis. But we cannot accept the solutions you are attempting to impose.

In the United States, you have today created a law, the

Telecommunications Reform Act, which repudiates your own Constitution and insults the dreams of Jefferson, Washington, Mill, Madison, DeToqueville, and Brandeis. These dreams must now be born anew in us.

You are terrified of your own children, since they are natives in a world where you will always be immigrants. Because you fear them, you entrust your bureaucracies with the parental responsibilities you are too cowardly to confront yourselves. In our world, all the sentiments and expressions of humanity, from the debasing to the angelic, are parts of a seamless whole, the global conversation of bits. We cannot separate the air that chokes from the air upon which wings beat.

In China, Germany, France, Russia, Singapore, Italy and the United States, you are trying to ward off the virus of liberty by erecting guard posts at the frontiers of Cyberspace. These may keep out the contagion for a small time, but they will not work in a world that will soon be blanketed in bit-bearing media.

Your increasingly obsolete information industries would perpetuate themselves by proposing laws, in America and elsewhere, that claim to own speech itself throughout the world. These laws would declare ideas to be another industrial product, no more noble than pig iron. In our world, whatever the human mind may create can be reproduced and distributed infinitely at no cost. The global conveyance of thought no longer requires your factories to accomplish.

These increasingly hostile and colonial measures place us in the same position as those previous lovers of freedom and self-determination who had to reject the authorities of distant, uninformed powers. We must declare our virtual selves immune to your sovereignty, even as we continue to consent to your rule over our bodies. We will spread ourselves across the Planet so that no one can arrest our thoughts.

We will create a civilization of the Mind in Cyberspace. May it be more humane and fair than the world your governments have made before.

# Appendix 4: Web Resources

**The West Virginia Textbook War:**

https://americanradioworks.publicradio.org/features/textbooks/

**Tor:**

Tor Project: https://www.torproject.org/

Tor Deanonymization Methods:
https://www.google.com/search?as_q=tor+deanonymization&as_sitesearch=youtube.com

**I2P:**

Get I2P: https://geti2p.net/en/

Practical attacks against I2P:
https://sites.cs.ucsb.edu/~chris/research/doc/raid13_i2p.pdf

**LokiNet:**

Project page: https://lokinet.org/

**WireGuard:**

Project page: https://www.wireguard.com/

**Shadowsocks:**

Project Page: https://shadowsocks.org/

**Project Geneva:**

GitHub Repository: https://github.com/kkevsterrr/geneva

**Yggdrasil:**

Project page: https://yggdrasil-network.github.io/

**Serval Mesh:**

Project page: https://servalproject.org/

**Firechat Articles:**

The Guardian:
https://www.google.co.uk/search?as_q=FireChat&as_sitesearch=www.theguardian.com

The Conversation:
https://www.google.co.uk/search?as_q=FireChat&as_sitesearch=theconversation.com

Times of India:
https://www.google.co.uk/search?as_q=FireChat&as_sitesearch=timesofindia.indiatimes.com

**Briar:**

https://briarproject.org/

**Element:**

https://element.io/

**Session:**

https://getsession.org/

**White Mouse:**

https://whitemouse.chat/

**Wifi Mesh Networking:**

Guifi (Spain) https://guifi.net/en/what_is_guifinet

Freifunk (Germany) https://freifunk.net/en/

Coolab (Brazil) https://www.coolab.org/

PYMESH (India) https://pymeshnet.gitlab.io/

**Starlink Articles:**

Ookla.com: https://www.google.co.uk/search?as_q=starlink&as_sitesearch=ookla.com

The Register: https://www.google.co.uk/search?as_q=starlink&as_sitesearch=w

ww.theregister.com

The Verge:
https://www.google.co.uk/search?as_q=starlink&as_sitesearch=w
ww.theverge.com

The Intercept:
https://www.google.co.uk/search?as_q=starlink&as_sitesearch=t
heintercept.com

**Collateral Freedom:**

Open Internet Tools Project:
https://web.archive.org/web/20130718065958/http://openitp.or
g/pdfs/CollateralFreedom.pdf

Open Technology Fund:
https://www.opentech.fund/results/supported-
projects/greatfire-expanding-collateral-freedom/

Reporters Without Borders:
https://web.archive.org/web/20170104165310/https://12mars.rs
f.org/2016-en/collateral-freedom-how-we-are-doing-it/

GreatFire.org:
https://www.google.co.uk/search?as_q=collateral+freedom&as_s
itesearch=greatfire.org

**Refraction Networking:**

Refraction.network: https://refraction.network/

TapDance (paper 1):
https://www.usenix.org/system/files/conference/foci17/foci17-
paper-frolov_0.pdf

TapDance (paper 2):
https://refraction.network/papers/deployment-pets20.pdf

**Network Censorship Metrics:**

NetBlocks: https://netblocks.org/

Open Observatory of Network Interference(OONI):
https://ooni.org

**Censorship Research or News:**

CensorBib: https://censorbib.nymity.ch/

BleepingComputer:
https://www.bleepingcomputer.com/tag/censorship/

Bruce Schneier: https://www.schneier.com/

AppleCensorship: https://applecensorship.com/

The Conversation:
https://theconversation.com/us/search?q=censorship

**Network Hijacks and Reroutes:**

Ars Technica:
https://www.google.co.uk/search?as_q=bgp+hijack&as_sitesearch=arstechnica.com

The Register:
https://www.google.co.uk/search?as_q=bgp+hijack&as_sitesearch=theregister.com

**Ukrainian Internet Reroutes:**

Wired:
https://www.google.co.uk/search?as_q=ukraine+internet+reroute&as_sitesearch=wired.com

## ABOUT THE AUTHOR

Philip G. Collier is a career professional in the airline industry, holding the ATP certificate in three countries, with multiple type ratings. He has been a radio enthusiast since the mid 1970s and enjoys writing about radio, travel, and piloting the heavy jets. He is enthusiastic about free and open source software and has published popular operating systems based on GNU/Linux. He is strongly against internet censorship and promotes circumvention technologies in operating systems such as *MOFO Linux*. A webmaster since 2006, Collier has been running websites which help people improve their lives through computing and radio technology. He says, "Once you learn how to learn, you can change your life. Nobody will tell you, but that is the truth. Truth will indeed set you free."